OUTRAGEOUS CHINESE

A Guide to Chinese Street Language

by James J. Wang

China Books & Periodicals, Inc.
San Francisco

First Edition, October 1994

Library of Congress Catalog Card Number: 94-94622

ISBN 0-8351-2532-7

Printed in the United States of America by:
China Books & Periodicals, Inc.
The Chinese characters in this book were created using the Apple Chinese Language Kit in the Song font. The English font with diacritical marks was created by Diane Hume of Electric Dragon.

To Rainbow Chen, for her stubborn love and unlimited generosity to give me away to the United States, where this book was born.

Acknowledgments

I am indiscriminate in choosing friends, which is unacceptable to most Chinese. They say, "A man is known by the company he keeps." I have been skeptical about this saying since childhood. What if I have two totally different friends, one, a famous professor of religion, and the other, a guy that has been in and out of jail many times for sexual harassment? They may say, "Well, then you may have dual personality." Fine, whatever they say. They may partly be right. I use "partly" here because I believe dual personality is not enough to paint a picture of me. I have a weird personality that radiates in all directions.

Because of my indiscriminate nature, I've got friends — real friends — of every description. They are all nice to me and find me great company to keep. They all talk differently, which has enriched my repertoire of Chinese and contributed to the birth of this book. I wish all my friends, men and women, in China, could hear my sincere thank-you.

I feel deeply indebted to Greg Jones and Lisa Wichser. Without their encouragement, enlightening ideas and editorial assistance, this project would never have been possible.

A special thank-you goes to Chris Noyes and Margareta Noyes, who provided me with everything I needed to write this book.

Thanks go to Professor Cornelius C. Kubler of Williams College, Professor Zhao Qiguang of Carleton College and Rebecca Weiner, author of *Living in China* for their contributions to the book.

Finally, I want to thank my good friends Yi Mu, author of *Crisis at Tiananmen* and Lisa Ryan for proofreading the manuscript, Wendy K. Lee for book design and Linda Revel for cover design.

James J. Wang

San Francisco, USA
August 1, 1994

Contents

Publisher's Foreword

This book is intended to provide the student of modern Mandarin Chinese (*Putonghua*) with access to vocabulary, idioms and slang that have never been taught in the classroom and would rarely be seen in respectable literature, but have high usage in every-day informal speech. Books such as this exist in all other major languages — we hope this fills the gap for Chinese. We hope not to put off those readers who are offended by vulgarities or obscenities in Chinese or in English, but feel it is important to recognize these terms when hearing them spoken in China. We would caution against using them except in situations where appropriate.

Similarly, those discussions on sex, drugs, bribery, and other risky ventures is in no way intended to encourage such activities. Indeed, recognition of terms involved in these activities may be protection against misunderstandings and subsequent unwanted involvement. For example, if a woman on the street offers to fix a man's pants (see Chapter 6), she may not be a seamstress!

We have chosen to use many English obscenities in translating the Chinese terms in order to demon-strate their shock value. Students are advised to consider appropriate usage for these terms much as they would in Western society. When in doubt, it is best not to try using questionable language.

Readers of this book should note that it is written by a young, well-educated man from Beijing, with much exposure to Western influences. The examples of dialogue and vocabulary he has chosen reflect language he has heard. Other Chinese of different ages, regions and backgrounds may or may not use all of these terms. China is a large country with many different people. The author has intended merely to introduce these words, entertain the readers and spur students on to learn more, and not provide a comprehensive, scholarly volume on all possible slang vocabulary.

The Chinese characters for most of the terms used are included, but in some cases usage of slang or vulgar terms is not standard and there may be variant written characters.

The text assumes the reader has at least an introductory knowledge of modern Chinese pronunciation. If not, please read Appendix A for a brief introduction or review.

Finally, thanks to the many teachers, translators, and students who have encouraged us in this book. Some are mentioned in the text, many are not. Some of their suggestions have been incorporated into this book.

Thanks also to the good folks at Tengu Books whose publication of *Japanese Street Slang* gave us the courage to do this volume.

Suggestions for other terms and usage that may be used in future editions are welcomed by the author and publisher.

Chapter 1

DANGEROUS CHINESE

Some of the words or combinations of words in the Chinese language must be spoken with caution and care, or you will find yourself in a very awkward, embarrassing situation.

1. Importance of tones

Foreigners learning Chinese usually have a hard time with the four tones of the language*, and so do Chinese not brought up in urban areas of north China. Here are some stories to illustrate the importance of tones.

When I was a student at Beijing University, I had a classmate from the countryside of Shaanxi province. He had a strong accent when speaking Mandarin Chinese and was very much frustrated by the four tones. One time in the classroom, we were all doing English grammar exercises. It was very quiet. Suddenly, he asked the female student by his side,

"Something's wrong with my pen. May I use yours?"
我的笔坏了了,可以借用你的笔吗?
Wǒ de bǐ huài le, kéyǐ jìe yòng nǐ de bǐ ma?

Everybody was astonished at first and then laughed loudly. The girl was so embarrassed, her face turned red down to her neck.

* See Appendix for discussion of the four tones.

"Why are you laughing?" shouted Mr. Bad Pronunciation. This set all the students there laughing even more heartily.

It turned out that on account of his difficulty with the four tones, he mispronounced the word for "pen" (*bǐ*). Instead of saying it correctly in the third tone, he used the first tone. Pronounced in the first tone, *bī* is the slang term for a vagina, the equivalent of the English word "pussy" or "cunt". So his sentence became "Something's wrong with my pussy. May I use yours?"

❅ ❅ ❅

Michelle was from the United States. She had been studying Chinese for two years in Taiwan and two years at the Beijing Language Institute before she was employed as an English editor by a foreign language publisher in Beijing. She and I worked in the same office. She talked to me in Chinese whenever there was a chance for practice.

One morning she asked me in Chinese, "Do you want to have sex?"

My heart skipped a beat. "What do you mean?" I asked.

"Do - you - want - to - have - sex?" she said more slowly and emphatically. To tell the truth, I really wanted to say "yes", but I was not sure if she meant it. So I said, "Would you write down what you said?"

"Sure," she said. So she wrote,

"Are you religious?"
你信教吗？
Nǐ xìn jiào ma?

on a piece of paper. "No," I said at once. She confused "believe in religion" (信 教 *xìn jiào*) with "sexual intercourse" (性交 *xìng jiāo*). (Pay attention to the two different tone marks of *jiào* 教 and *jiāo* 交.)

❊ ❊ ❊

There are a lot of similar stories involving the misuse of the four tones. Once an American missionary was praying in a church in China. He meant to say,

"Oh Lord, we love you!"
主啊！我们爱你！
Zhǔ a, wǒmen ài nǐ!

The people praying along with him could hardly refrain from laughing, because he pronounced the word for God (主 *zhǔ*) in the wrong tone, making it "pig" (猪 *zhū*).

I hope you will remember these stories and always pay attention to the four tones, and avoid embarrassment.

Bian Fan

Biàn fàn means "simple home-style meal." It's fine to say

"Please come to my home for a simple meal."
请你到我家吃一点便饭。
Qǐng nǐ dào wǒ jiā chī yīdiǎn biàn fàn.

But once one of my students, trying to be overpolite, added the word "little" (*xiǎo*), saying *Qǐng nǐ dào wǒ jiā chī yīdiǎn xiǎo biàn fàn.* The problem is *xiǎo biàn* means "pee, urine". So what the student really said was "Please come over to my house and have a little urine food!"

2. Embarrassing combinations of characters

A lot of Chinese are in the habit of ending their imperative sentences with *ba* (吧). For instance,

Let's go.
走吧。
Zǒu ba.

Time to eat.
吃饭吧。
Chī fàn ba.

Let's get started.
开始吧。
Kāi shǐ ba.

Mastery of the usage of the character *ba* is very important in learning Chinese. But you must be very careful when the word is preceded by characters with the pronunciation of *jī* or *wáng*.

Chinese like chicken. Most of the time when they treat a guest to dinner, chicken is served. Also Chinese like to keep reminding the guest to help him or herself to whatever is on the table, especially to the dishes that they think are exceptionally good. So when they ask their guest to eat some chicken, they would often say,

"Please eat chicken."
吃鸡吧。
Chī jī ba.

The speaker usually doesn't realize what's wrong until everybody else at the table smiles or grins mysteriously or starts laughing, because *jī ba* (鸡 吧) has the same pronunciation as *jība* (鸡 巴), which is the slang word for "penis" in Chinese, the equivalent of "cock" or "dick" in English. If the guest is a fun person who likes to crack jokes, he would say,

"I don't eat cock. I only eat chicken."
我不吃鸡巴。我只吃鸡。
Wǒ bù chī jība. Wǒ zhǐ chī jī.

When you need to say something about a TV set (电视机 *diànshì jī*), transistor radio (收音机 *shōu yīn jī*), tape recorder (录音机 *lù yīn jī*), or anything with the sound of *jī* at the end, try to avoid using *ba* after it.

❄ ❄ ❄

When the Chinese get a phone call, they like to guess who the receiver is. If the receiver happens to be surnamed *Wáng* (王), they would often ask,

You are Xiao (Lao) Wang, aren't you?
你是小 (老) 王吧?
Nǐ shì xiǎo (lǎo) wáng ba?

This should be avoided, because *wáng bā* (王 八), which is pronounced the same as *wáng ba* in the above sentence, literally means turtle in Chinese. It is used to indicate a cuckolded husband, for the Chinese believe that female turtles are promiscuous by nature.

Buy and Sell

Buy and sell (买卖 *mǎi* and *mài*) are so confusing in meaning, writing, and pronunciation, even native Chinese speakers make mistakes quite frequently. Mastery of the difference can save you from a lot of dangerous situations, especially when you work as a commercial interpreter. Both look very much alike and have the same *pinyin* romanization, but with different tones.

I used to have difficulty distinguishing *mǎi* from *mài*. I didn't know which was which in writing. My Chinese teacher gave me a simple way to discern the difference, which I hope will be useful to you. What he said was:

mǎi (买) is buy, because you don't have anything on the top, and you have to buy it; *mài* (卖) is sell, because you have something on the top, and you can sell it.

3. Careful shopping

When shopping for meat in the Chinese free market, people should not bargain using the following phrases, which are often used by Chinese themselves and sometimes result in a quarrel.

Your meat is too expensive.
你的肉挺贵嘛。
Nǐ de ròu tǐng guì ma.

Your meat is very cheap.
你的肉挺便宜嘛。
Nǐ de ròu tǐng piányi ma.

In the Chinese language, there is no difference between "meat" and "flesh" as there is in English and the character 肉 (*ròu*) means both animal meat and human flesh. The above statements sound very offensive to some meat vendors. If they happen to have very bad sales that day and are in a bad mood, they might retort,

> "It is your damned mother's flesh that is expensive!"
> 你他妈的肉才贵呢！
> *Nǐ tā mā de ròu cái guì ne!* *

or

> "It is your damned mother's flesh that is cheap!"
> 你他妈的肉才便宜呢！
> *Nǐ tā mā de ròu cái piányi ne!*

If the buyer fights back in stronger words, a quarrel or even a fist fight may result. If this happens to you, the best strategy is to say sorry to the vendor and then tell him or her that what you really meant to say is "the meat you are selling (你卖的肉 *nǐ mài de ròu*) is cheap."

*For the usage of *ta ma de*, please see Chapter 4.

An American diplomat was taking a language test and wanted to compliment the female Chinese examiner on her pretty handbag. He said:

> "Your foreskin is really pretty!"
> 你的包皮真好看！
> *Nǐ de bāopí zhēn hǎo kàn!*

What he should have said, of course was

> "Your handbag is really pretty!"
> 你的皮包真好看！
> *Nǐ de píbāo zhēn hǎo kàn!*

Distinguish carefully: *píbāo* (handbag, purse) and *bāopí* (foreskin).

4. Taking a name in Chinese

If you need a Chinese name, it is best to consult a Chinese person who knows the Chinese language very well, because it is not easy to find a good Chinese name.

Many Chinese have names they themselves hate to be called. For example, a lot of Chinese whose surname is *Yáng* (杨) are named *Yáng Wěi* (杨 伟). As far as I know, there are literally hundreds of thousands of people with that name. The reason their parents give them such a name is that they want their children to be great (*wěi* 伟 meaning "great" in Chinese). But they don't realize that *Yáng Wěi* (扬 伟) is just homonymous with sexual impotence (阳 萎) in Chinese. This name has become a joke. Every time a teacher takes a roll call and that name is called, both the teacher and students giggle and try their best to refrain from laughing. Even after marriage, the wife might crack jokes about her husband's name, and say,

Are you really impotent?
你真的阳萎吗？
Nǐ zhēn de yángwěi ma?

❀　❀　❀

Foreigners who choose to have surnames like *Zhū* (朱), *Niú* (牛), or *Mǎ* (马) should be careful in selecting personal names.

Zhū has the same pronunciation as "pig" (猪) in Chinese. So don't name yourself *Zhū Wěi* (朱伟) or *Zhū Xīn* (朱心) because *Zhū Wěi* is homonymous with "pig's tail", and *Zhū Xīn*, "pig's heart".

Don't name yourself *Niú Wěi* (牛伟) or *Niú Fèn* (牛奋), because *niú* means ox in Chinese; *Niú Wěi* is homonymous with ox tail and *Niú Fèn* , ox excretions.

So the best way to get a good Chinese name is to ask a literate Chinese friend to choose one for you.

What's in a Name?

1. An American by the name of Silver was accidentally named Si Leren. But this sounds like *sǐ le rén*, meaning "a person has died."

2. An American by the name of Valenzuela was accidentally named Fan Sile. This sounds like *fán sǐ le*, meaning "incredibly annoying".

3. An American by the name of Vaden was accidentally named Wei Teng. But this sounds like *wèi téng*, meaning "stomach hurts".

5. Commenting on a hairstyle

When someone has a haircut or a new hairstyle, his colleagues or friends like to make some comments on it and, more often than not, ask about the price. They might remark,

"How much is your head? Where did you get it? Not bad!"
你这头多少钱？在哪儿理的？理得不错嘛 ！
Nǐ zhè tóu duō shǎo qián? Zài nǎr lǐ de? Lǐ de bú cuò ma!

or

"Your head is pretty. What's the price?"
你这头很漂亮。多少钱？
Nǐ zhè tóu hěn piàoliang. Duōshǎo qián?

The speaker might not realize that this is not the proper way to comment on a hairstyle, because a lot of people speak that way. Even so, some people still don't like to be asked about the price of their head. Actually it is the same mistake as "how much is your flesh?" When you really want to comment on a hairstyle or haircut, the following phrases might be helpful.

hairstyle: 发 型 *fàxíng*

the shape of head: 头 型 *tóuxíng*

haircut: 理 发 *lǐfà*

hair: 头 发 *tóufà*

This hairstyle suits you perfectly.
这个发型很适合你。
Zhège fàxíng hěn shìhé nǐ.

It is a nice haircut. How much did it cost?
头发理得很好。花了多少钱？
Tóufà lǐ de hěn hǎo. Huā le duōshǎo qián?

You look better after a haircut.
你理发后显得很精神。
Nǐ lǐfà hòu xiǎn de hěn jīngshen.

Your hair looks like it has been bitten by a dog.
(Your hair is very badly cut.)
你的头发理得象狗啃过似的。
Nǐ de tóufà lǐ de xiàng gǒu kěn guò shì de.

6. Importance of correct pronunciation

A lot of people have difficulty pronouncing the numbers 7, 8 correctly in a telephone number. They pronounce 7, 8 not *qī bā* but *jī bā*, which is the slang word for "penis".

Once an American friend of mine left a message on the answering machine when I was in China.

Please call me back. My phone number is 778-7878.
请给我回电话。我的电话号码是鸡鸡巴鸡巴鸡巴。
Qǐng gěi wǒ huí diànhuà. Wǒ de diànhuà hào mǎ shì jī jī bā jī bā jī bā (778-7878).

Of course, I knew pretty well what he meant by his phone number. But if he happened to give a woman this *jiba-jiba* phone number, I wonder how she would react.

❊ ❊ ❊

In 1987 during a beauty pageant in Hong Kong, the M.C. asked one of the contestants what kind of personality she had. She answered in Shanghai-accented Mandarin with great confidence,

"I am open and above-board, without any pubic hair."

我光明正大, 没有阴毛。

Wǒ guāng míng zhèng dà, méiyǒu yīn máo.

A lot of Shanghai people told me that it was a disgrace and that she let them down. What the contestant really meant to say was that she "never plots against anyone" (没有阴谋 *méiyǒu yīnmóu*). But people in southern China often pronounce *yīn móu* 阴谋 (conspiracy) *yīn máo* 阴毛 (pubic hair) in their dialect. She is very beautiful and is now a well-known movie star. Every time I see her on screen, her "no pubic hair" confession just spontaneously comes to my mind.

Chapter 2

WHAT DO I CALL YOU?

1. What do I call you?

Americans, men and women, old and young, like to be called by their first name. With the Chinese, the form of address is much more complicated. It will definitely be deemed disrespectful if a young person calls an old person by his or her first name. So the following points are worthy of notice.

(1) Men and women more or less the same age call each other either by their full name, nickname, or surname preceded by "old" (老 lǎo) or "little" (小 xiǎo) according to their age. They seldom call each other by their first name. The first names are usually used by family members, relatives or sometimes by friends. If you call somebody by his or her first name, whom you don't know very well, people will think you are trying to be intimate.

(2) Chinese names consist of either three characters or two characters. When you need to call somebody who has a two-character name, you always should call them by their full name or surname preceded by "old" (老 lǎo) or "little" (小 xiǎo). They should never be called by their first name, not even by their closest friends. Their first name is used only by their lovers. For example, a woman is named Li Hong. Nobody is supposed to call her Hong, except for her lover or husband, because a one-syllable name

sounds very intimate.

(3) The young call the old by their surnames followed by uncle (叔叔 *shūshu* or 伯伯 *bóbo*), aunt (阿姨 *āyí*), grandpa (爷爷 *yéye*) or grandmother (奶奶 *nǎinai*) on non-business occasions, or surnames preceded by "old" (老 *lǎo*) or followed by "Mr." (先生 *xiānsheng*) on formal or business occasions. For example, if an old person is named Wang Zheng, and he is about the age of your parents, you should call him Uncle Wang (王伯伯 *wáng bóbo* or 王叔叔 *wáng shūshu*) on casual occasions, and old Wang (老王 *lǎo wáng*) or Mr. Wang (王先生 *wáng xiāngsheng*) on business occasions. Never call the old by their first name.

(4) Sometimes highly respected old people are called by their surname followed by "old" (老 *lǎo*) to show esteem, such as 陈老 *chén lǎo*, i.e., Venerable Chen.

(5) Students at all levels usually call each other by their full name. Two-character first names are sometimes used between friends. Teachers are not supposed to call their students by their first name, and only full names are allowed.

(6) Young people in Beijing often greet each other by saying "Hi, buddy!" (哥们儿 *gē menr*), even when they don't know each other.

Don't write notes or letters to your Chinese friends in red ink, because it means severance of friendship. Writing in any other color is fine.

---

2. Greetings

When people who know each other meet, they often exchange "Hellos!" (你好! *Nǐ hǎo!*). In most parts of China people are not used to greeting each other good morning, good afternoon or good evening. They seem to use *nǐ hǎo* all the time. In many places people greet each other "morning" (早 *zǎo*) in the morning, meaning exactly the same as "good morning" in English. It is okay if you say good afternoon (下午好 *xiàwu hǎo*) to an acquaintance, but it doesn't sound like authentic Chinese.

The exchange of *"nǐ hǎo"* is usually followed by

"Have you had your meal?"
(你)吃过了吗？
(Nǐ) chī guò le ma?

Often in Chinese history people struggled for enough food to eat, and they had to spend most of their time thinking about how and where they could find food for the next meal. This is probably how this kind of greeting came into being. If you happen to be asked if you've had your meal, don't take it as an invitation to dinner. Just regard it as a casual greeting.

Sometimes *"nǐ hǎo"* is followed by

"Where are you going?"
去哪儿？ or 干吗去？
Qù nǎr? or *Gàn má qù?*

If you don't want it to be known where you are going, just say,

> "I am walking around aimlessly (blindly)," or "I am just hanging out."
> 瞎溜达。
> *Xiā liū da. (Xiā* means "blindly".)

Please note the following dialog which takes place at a party. It will be very useful to you. All the sentences included are very colloquial and idiomatic.

A: Hi! Long time no see. How are you doing?
你好！好久不见了。混得怎么样？
Nǐ hǎo! Hǎo jiǔ bú jiàn le. Hùn de zěnme yàng?

B: Well, I'm hanging out. You've got a rosy complexion. Aren't you a little bit fatter?
咳，瞎混。你气色不错。是不是胖点儿了？
Hāi, xiā hùn. Nǐ qì sè bú cuò. Shì bú shì pàng diǎnr le?

A: That is possible. I have not been that busy lately. I have nothing to do but eat and sleep.
有可能。最近我不怎么忙。吃了睡，睡了吃。
Yǒu kěnéng. Zuìjìn wǒ bù zěnme máng. Chī le shuì, shuì le chī.

B: That's really great! I envy you very much. I have to work like cows and horses every day.
那多好。真羡慕你。我每天都得作牛作马。
Nà duō hǎo. Zhēn xiànmù nǐ. Wǒ měi tiān dōu de zuò niú zuò mǎ.

A: Take it easy. Don't work too hard, or your health will be ruined.

悠着点儿。别累坏了身子。

Yōu zhe diǎnr. Bié lèi huài le shēnzi.

B: That would never happen. Thank you for your concern.

不会的。谢谢你的关心。

Bú huì de. Xièxie nǐ de guānxīn.

3. Asking about age

People in China, except for some of the women in their 30s, don't feel offended or unhappy when asked about their age. Usually they will tell you how old they are. There are some tactful ways to find out a woman's age even if she doesn't want to tell the truth. Just guess her age by deducting five to ten years from the age that you really think she is and she will be very, very happy. Before she realizes it, she would respond by saying something like

Do I really look so young?

我真的显得那么年青吗？

Wǒ zhēn de xiǎn de nàme niánqīng ma?

This answer gives her away — she must be older than the age you guessed!

For different aged people, the ways of asking about their age should be different. To a child, you should ask,

What is your age?
你几岁了？
Nǐ jǐ suì le?

or

How old are you?
多大了？
Duō dà le?

To the aged, the question should be put like

What is your respectable age?
您多大岁数了？
Nín duō dà suì shù le?

The best way, I think, to ask a person any age is

In which year were you born?
你哪年生的？
Nǐ nǎ nián shēng de?

您哪年生人？
Nín nǎ nián shēng rén?

or

Under which astrological sign were you born?
你属什么的？
Nǐ shǔ shénme de? *

By so asking you can do the calculation yourself and know exactly how old the person is, as some of the Chinese tell their age by Chinese reckoning, namely, adding one year or two years to their actual age.

---

*Each Chinese year has the name of one of twelve animals, namely, the Rat, Ox, Tiger, Rabbit, Dragon, Snake, Horse, Ram, Monkey, Rooster, Dog and Boar. The years run in cycles so that the same animal-year recurs every twelve years.

Never use *nǐ jǐ suì?* (你几岁？) to ask about an old person's age, because "几" (*jǐ*) is used when asking about numbers under 10.

Yours or mine?

Be careful always to get your pronunciation straight. If you are asked a question with "you" (你 *nǐ*), the answer ordinarily will be with "I" (我 *wǒ*), not with "you" (你 *nǐ*).

During a Chinese language examination over which I once presided, the female Chinese examiner asked the pregnant female American examinee about her baby:

"Do you want to feed it mother's milk or cow's milk?"
你要喂他母奶还是牛奶？
Nǐ yào wèi tā mǔ nǎi hái shì niú nǎi?

When the examinee didn't understand *mǔ nǎi*, the examiner rephrased her question:

"Do you want to feed her your milk or cow's milk?"
你要喂他你的奶还是牛的奶？
Nǐ yào wèi tā nǐ de nǎi hái shì niú de nǎi?

To which the examinee responded without missing a beat:

"Oh, I want to feed her your milk."
哦，我要喂他你的奶。
Wǒ yào wèi tā nǐ de nǎi.

4. Dear or Honey

When writing in Chinese to someone in China, don't use "Dear" (亲爱的 *qīn ài de*) in the salutation, because it would make the addressee very uneasy and she or he might think you are weird and strange, trying to be overly intimate. Just use the surname followed by Mr. (先生 *xiānsheng*), Ms. (女士 *nǚshì*) or Miss (小姐 *xiǎojie*), or "old" (老 *lǎo*) followed by the surname when the addressee is older than you and "little" (小 *xiǎo*) when the addressee is younger. If you write to a person who you think is highly respectable, you should add "Respectable" (尊敬的 *zūnjìng de*).

In the Chinese language, "Dear" (亲爱的 *qīn ài de*) is only used between loved ones such as parents and children, lovers, husbands and wives.

Always remember to use *qīn ài de* (亲爱的) on someone you literally love!

When writing business reports or letters to your boss or people in a higher position than you, you should use "Respectable" (尊敬的 *zūnjìng de*) or "Beloved" (敬爱的 *jìng ài de*) instead of "Dear" (亲爱的 *qīn ài de*).

When a man needs to speak about his wife, he could refer to her in the following ways:

My:

> *qīzi* 妻子 (Used on all occasions.)
>
> *lǎopo* 老婆 (Used on formal occasions.)
>
> *àiren* 爱人 (Mostly used in Mainland China on all occasions.)
>
> *tàitai* 太太 (Used on all occasions.)
>
> *xífur* 媳妇儿 (Mostly used in North China. Colloquial.)
>
> *nèi ren* 内人 (Mostly used by older generation in North China. Sounds old-fashioned.)
>
> *xián nèi zhù* 贤内助 (Complimentary way to call one's wife.)
>
> *jiā lǐ nèi wèi* 家里那位 (Colloquial.)
>
> *háizi tā mā* 孩子他妈 (Child's or children's mother) (Coloquial. Mostly used in northern rural areas.)
>
> *nǚren* 女人 (Mostly used in the countryside.)

A woman calls her husband my:

> *zhàngfu* 丈夫 (Used on all occasions.)
>
> *lǎo gōng* 老公 (Colloquial. Mostly used in South China.)
>
> *xiānsheng* 先生 (Used on all occasions.)
>
> *àiren* 爱人 (Mostly used in Mainland China on all occasions.)
>
> *háizi tā bà* 孩子他爸 (Child's or children's father) (Colloquial. Mostly used in northern rural areas.)
>
> *nánren* 男人 (Mostly used in the countryside.)

Chapter 3

LOVE AND SEX

1. Inexpressible love

One of my best American friends once told me that when he was studying Chinese, he was taught to say "I hotly love you" (我热爱你 *Wǒ rè ài nǐ*) to express hot love for someone. Actually the Chinese never use "hotly love" (热爱 *rè ài*) to show personal love. Instead, they say,

I love you very much.
我非常爱你。
Wǒ fēicháng ài nǐ.

or

My love for you is burning hot.
我爱你爱得发烫。
Wǒ ài nǐ ài de fā tàng.

热爱 *rè ài* (literally meaning "to hotly love") is only used on an idolized object. You can say "hotly love motherland" (热爱祖国 *rè ài zǔguó*) or "hotly love one's career" (热爱事业 *rè ài shìyè*). During the Cultural Revolution, the personality cult was all the rage, and all the people had to say "hotly love Chairman Mao" (热爱毛主席 *rè ài máo zhǔxí*).

Chinese people are still circumspect about love, at least on the surface. In most cases, lovers don't say "I love you" (我爱你 *Wǒ ài nǐ*) to each other. They think love should be cherished in the heart and cannot be expressed in words. Many couples have not said "I love you" in their whole lifetime together. As far as I know, many lovers only say "I love you" when they are in the middle of a extremely passionate kiss or at the moment of reaching an orgasm. But when they write each other, they present a totally different picture, full of words of love and other endearments.

Rather than say "I love you", there are many other ways to show love for each other, such as a smile, a gesture, sending a meaningful gift, etc. There are also some indirect ways to express loving feelings. Here are some examples:

I am thinking of you from morning till night.
我从早到晚都在想你。
Wǒ cóng zǎo dào wǎn dōu zài xiǎng nǐ.

I cannot get you off my mind.
我想你想得不能自拔。
Wǒ xiǎng nǐ xiǎng de bù néng zì bá.

All my dreams are about you.
我梦里全是你。
Wǒ mèng lǐ qúan shì nǐ.

I had a dream last night. I dreamed of being with you. You told me you love me and I said I love you. Is that true?
昨晚我做了一个梦。我梦见你我在一起。你说你爱我，我说我爱你。是这样吗？
Zuó wǎn wǒ zuò le yí gè mèng. Wǒ mèng jiàn nǐ wǒ zài yì qǐ. Nǐ shuō nǐ ài wǒ, wǒ shuō wǒ ài nǐ. Shì zhèyàng ma?

Everything of mine belongs to you.
我的一切都是你的。
Wǒ de yíqiè dōu shì nǐ de.

My heart has been given to you.
我的心已交给了你。
Wǒ de xīn yǐ jiāo gěi le nǐ.

2. Sexual terminology

There are a hundred and one ways to say "have sex" in Chinese. But it proves very hard for non-native Chinese speakers, even for some native speakers, to say it to the right person at the right time in the right place.

Suppose you go to a hospital and the doctor needs to know about your sex life for some reason. He should ask very indirectly,

Were you with your wife (husband) last night?
昨晚你和你太太 (先生)在一起吗？
Zuó wǎn nǐ hé nǐ tàitai (xiānshēng) zài yì qǐ ma?

He might be more specific,

Did the thing happen between you last night?
昨晚你们有事吗？
Zuó wǎn nǐmen yǒu shì ma?

Did you do the house thing last night?
昨晚你们有房事吗？
Zuó wǎn nǐmen yǒu fáng shì ma?

Did you stay in the same room (bed) last night?
昨晚你们同房 (床) 了吗？
Zuó wǎn nǐmen tóng fáng (chuáng) le ma?

If the doctor asks you,

"Did you have intercourse last night?"
昨晚你们性交了吗？
Zuó wǎn nǐmen xìng jiāo le ma?

it would sound very out of place and embarrass you.

The following lists are given to show when, where, and how to say "sexual intercourse."

(1) The terms listed below are mostly used in written Chinese:

sexual intercourse: 性交 *xìngjiāo*

intercourse of happiness: 交欢 *jiāo huān*

copulation: 交媾 *jiáo gòu*

combination of sexes: 交合 *jiāo hé*

sexual love: 性爱 *xìng ài*

clouds and rain: 云雨 *yún yǔ*

Before sexual intercourse, please put on a condom.
性交前，请戴上避孕套。
Xìng jiāo qián, qǐng dài shàng bì yùn tào.

The Chinese seldom talk about sexual love in public.
中国人很少在公共场合谈论性爱。
Zhōngguó rén hěn shǎo zài gōng gòng chǎng hé tán lùn xìng ài.

(2) The following four terms may be used both in written and spoken Chinese:

house thing (thing done inside the house):
房事 *fáng shì*

go to bed (with): 上床 *shàng chuáng*

sleep (with): 睡觉 *shuìjiào*

make love: 做爱 or 造爱 *zuò ài* or *zào ài*

Examples:

When I pushed the door open, they were caught making love.
我推开门时，他们正在做爱。
Wǒ tuī kāi mén shí, tāmen zhèng zài zuò ài.

Women shouldn't have sex when they are having their period.
女人来例假时，不应有房事。
Nǚrén lái lì jià shí, bù yīng yǒu fáng shì.

(3) *Gàn* (干) is a colloquial word for "make love" or "do it" in Chinese. For example, you could ask a person,

"Have you ever made love?"
你们干过吗？
Nǐmen gàn guò ma?

(4) *Cào* (操) is the slang word for "have sex with" in Chinese, the equivalent of "screw" and "fuck" in English. It sounds very vulgar and is only used when you want to curse somebody or to show crudeness.

In China when a mother asks a daughter, a woman asks a woman, or a friend asks a friend about whether she or he has had sex with someone, the best way to ask should be:

Did you do that thing with him (her)?
你跟他(她)有事吗？
Nǐ gēn tā yǒu shì ma?

or

Did that happen between you?
你跟他有没有那个？
Nǐ gēn tā yǒu méi yǒu nèige?

When a buddy asks a buddy, he often says,

Did you go to bed with her?
你跟她上过床吗？
Nǐ gēn tā shàng guò chuáng ma?

Traditionally Chinese women only lost their virginity to their husband. It was taboo to have pre-marital sex. In present-day China people still value virginity, but they won't make a fuss about a woman that lost her virginity before marriage, thanks to the Western influence. This accounts for why the answer to the following riddle has changed.

Riddle: Which Chinese city is reminiscent of the "First Wedding Night" (新婚之夜 *xīn hūn zhī yè*)?
Original answer: Kaifeng 开封, a city in Henan province because *kāi fēng* means "unseal". It is often used to refer to opening of a box or a letter.

As a lot of women have had pre-marital sex, the newly wed husband doesn't expect to "see red" (见红 *jiàn hóng*) on the first wedding night, so the answer has changed to Haikou (海口). (*Hǎi kǒu:* seaport, a big opening; Haikou is the capital city of China's southernmost Hainan province.)

3. Love making

Chinese women are usually very shy during sex. Even after many years of marriage, they seldom initiate sex with their spouses. Besides, they seldom undress themselves for their husbands. It always seems to be their partner's job to take their clothes off. But after the love-making is over, they do compliment their partner on his virility. They often shower him with compliments like:

I feel on top of the world!
我好快活！
Wǒ hǎo kuàihuo!

You've got a real big dick! (Even if it's not very big.)
你的鸡鸡真大！
Nǐ de jīji zhēn dà.

You are simply great!
你真棒！
Nǐ zhēn bàng!

You are terrific in bed!
你的活儿真好！
Nǐ de huór zhēn hǎo!

I wish I had died in your arms.
刚才真想死在你的怀里。
Gāngcái zhēn xiǎng sǐ zài nǐ de huái lǐ.

Some other women may say:

You almost pierced me!
你差点儿把我捅 (弄)穿了。
Nǐ chà diǎnr bǎ wǒ tǒng (nòng) chuān le.

You are fantastic! How about one more time?
你太棒了。我还想来一回(次)。
Nǐ tài bàng le. Wǒ hái xiǎng lái yì huí (cì).

That thing of yours is really formidable, as hard as iron.
你那个真厉害！象铁一样。
Nǐ nèige zhēn lìhai! Xiàng tiě yí yàng.

Just like men in other countries, Chinese men like to be praised for their sexual prowess and to show off or brag about their virility. Done with love making, they may ask,

Have you counted how many thrusts I made just now?
刚才我干了多少下？
Gāngcái wǒ gàn le duō shǎo xià?

How long have we done it?
干了多长时间？
Gàn le duō cháng shíjiān?

Actually I could have gone longer, but I was afraid
I might hurt you.
其实我可以再干一会儿, 但我怕你受不了。
*Qí shí wǒ kéyǐ zài gàn yí huìr, dàn wǒ pà nǐ shòu bù
liǎo.*

If the man comes too fast or ejaculates prema-
turely, in most cases his partner just keeps quiet.
Sometimes she may say comforting words like,

"That's all right."
没关系。
Méi guānxi.

But some women do show their dissatisfaction. They
might say,

"How come you do it so fast? Really boring!"
怎么这么快? 真没劲!
Zěnme zhème kuài? Zhēn méi jìn!

When they are having their period, women in China often
say "bad luck" (倒霉 *dǎo méi*) or "regular vacation, period"
(例假 *lì jià*) instead of "menstruation" (月经 *yuèjīng*). For example, they would say,

"I am having bad luck." (I am having my period.)
我倒霉了.
Wǒ dǎo méi le.

I am having my period.
我来例假了.
Wǒ lái lì jià le.

Some words and sentences that might be used during male-female encounters are as follows:

condom: 避孕套 *bì yùn tào*

> Put on a condom. I don't want to be knocked up.
> 戴上避孕套。我可不想把肚子弄大。
> *Dài shàng bì yùn tào. Wǒ kě bù xiǎng bǎ dùzi nòng dà.*

coitus interruptus: 体外射精 *tǐ wài shè jīng*

the pill: 避孕药 *bì yùn yào*

IUD: 上环 *shàng huán*

> Man: Please allow me to put on a condom first.
> 让我先戴上避孕套。
> *Ràng wǒ xiān dài shàng bì yùn tào.*

> Woman: Unnecessary. I have an IUD.
> 不必了。我上环了。
> *Bú bì le. Wǒ shàng huán le.*

contraceptives: 避孕工具，避孕用品 *bì yùn gōngjù, bì yùn yòng pǐn*

menstruation: 月经 *yuèjīng*

be pregnant: 怀孕 *huái yùn*

Private Parts:

the very upper part of a penis: 龟头 *guī tóu* (*guī tóu* literally means "turtle head".)

foreskin: 包皮 *bāopí*

> Your foreskin is really long.
> 你的包皮真长！
> *Nǐ de bāopí zhēn cháng!*

vagina: 阴道 *yīndào*

clitoris: 阴蒂 *yīndì*

love button (the slang word for "clitoris" in Chinese): 爱扣 *ài kòu*

pubic hair: 阴毛 *yīnmáo*

breasts: 乳房 *rǔfáng*

tits: 奶子 *nǎizi* (the slang word for "breasts" in Chinese, it sounds vulgar.)

tits: 咪咪 *mīmi* (the slang word for "breasts" in Chinese, it sounds childish and funny.)

nipples: 奶头 *nǎitóu*

penis: 阴茎 *yīnjīng* (medical term)

penis, dick, cock: 鸡鸡, 鸡巴, 老二, 枪 *jīji, jība, lǎo èr, qiāng* (All are the slang words for "penis" in Chinese.)

toy: 玩艺儿 *wányìr* (the slang word for either female or male genitals)

little brother: 小弟弟 *xiǎo dìdi* (the slang word for "penis" in Chinese, it seems to be more used by women)

testicles: 睾丸 *gǎowán* (medical term)

balls: 蛋, 鸡巴蛋 *dàn, jība dàn* (the slang word for "testicles" in Chinese)

buttocks: 屁股 *pìgu*

hips: 臀部 *tún bù*

thigh: 大腿 *dà tuǐ*

anus: 肛门 *gāngmén*

butt eye: 屁眼 *pìyǎn* (vulgar term for "anus")

tongue: 舌头 *shétou*

Love-Making Terms:

embrace, hug: 拥抱 *yōngbào*

kiss: 亲嘴，亲吻，接吻 *qīn zuǐ, qīn wěn, jiē wěn*

French kiss: 深吻，法国式亲吻 *shēn wěn, fǎ guó shì qīn wěn*

stroke, fondle: 抚摸 *fǔ mō*

touch me: 摸我 *mō wǒ*

suck, eat: 吸 *xī*

full-figured, well-shaped, plump: 丰满 *fēngmǎn*

> Most full-figured women are sexy.
> 大多数丰满的女人都比较性感。
> *Dà duō shù fēngmǎn de nǚrén dōu bǐ jiào xìng gǎn.*

sexual desire, lust: 性欲 *xìngyù*

> I am sexually demanding.
> 我性欲很强。
> *Wǒ xìngyù hěn qiáng.*

sex appeal, sexy, voluptuous: 性感 *xìng gǎn*

bad breath: 口臭 *kǒu chòu*

> Your breath stinks.
> 你的嘴真臭。
> *Nǐ de zuǐ zhēn chòu.*

get wet: 湿了 *shī le*

erection, hard-on: 勃起，硬了 *bó qǐ, yìng le*

big: 大 *dà*

hard: 硬 *yìng*

soft: 软 *ruǎn*

sexual impotence, impotent: 阳萎 *yáng wěi*

fail to lift it up: 起不来 *qǐ bù lái* (the slang term for "impotence" in Chinese)

foreplay: 前戏 *qián xì*

make love: 做爱 *zuò ài*

love-making positions: 做爱姿势 *zuò ài zī shì*

> I am tired. Would you please get on top?
> 我累了, 你在上面好吗？
> *Wǒ lèi le, nǐ zài shàng miàn hǎo ma?*

> Is it all in?
> 都进去了吗？
> *Dōu jìn qù le ma?*

> Have you reached the spot?
> 顶到头了吗？
> *Dǐng dào tóu le ma?*

faster: 快点儿 *kuài diǎnr*

softer: 轻点儿 *qīng diǎnr*

climax, ecstasy: 高潮 *gāocháo*

come at the same time: 同时到达高潮 *tóngshí dào dá gāocháo*

premature ejaculation: 早泻 *zǎo xiè*

shoot, ejaculate: 射精 *shè jīng*

explode: 点炮 *diǎn pào* (the slang word for "ejaculation" in Chinese) come, shoot: 滋了 *zī le* (This slang word often means involuntary ejaculation.)

sperm: 精液 *jīngyè*

frigid: 性冷淡 *xìng lěngdàn*

overindulgence in sex: 房事过度 *fáng shì guò dù*

finger: 手指 *shǒu zhǐ*

> Would you please use your fingers first?
> 先用手弄一下好吗？
> *Xiān yòng shǒu nòng yíxià hǎo ma?*

male sexual instruments: 阳具, 阳器 *yáng jù, yáng qì*

aphrodisiac: 春药 *chūn yào* (lit., "Spring Medicine")

> You are really powerful! It looks like you have taken aphrodisiacs.
> 你真厉害, 象吃了春药似的。
> *Nǐ zhēn lìhai, xiàng chī le chūn yào sì de.*

masturbation, hand-job: 手淫, 手交 *shǒu yín, shǒu jiāo*

oral copulation: 口淫, 口交 *kǒu yín, kǒu jiāo*

anal sex: 肛交 *gāng jiāo*

virgin: 处女 *chù nǔ*

virgin: 童子, 童男 *tóng zǐ, tóng nán* (indicating a man who has never had sex before)

sex hungry: 性饥渴 *xìng jīkě*

sexually active, sexually demanding: 性欲强的 *xìngyù qiáng de*

hot and horny: 色迷迷的 *sè mí mí de*

sex life, love life: 性生活，爱情生活 *xìng shēnghuó, ài qíng shēnghuó*

extramarital affairs, extramarital love: 婚外恋 *hūn wài liàn*

sadist, sadism: 虐待狂 *nüè dài kuáng*

masochist, masochism: 受虐狂 *shòu nüè kuáng*

In colloquial Mandarin Chinese (both in Taiwan and mainland China), the erect penis is sometimes described as "at twelve o'clock" (十二点 *shí èr diǎn*) (as the hands of a clock are when they are pointing up straight at 12:00), while the flaccid penis is referred to as "half past six" (六点半 *liù diǎn bàn*).

---

4. Birth Control

China is the most populous country in the world, with a population of over 1.2 billion. Family planning is the country's state policy. Each couple is allowed to have only one child, although some couples in the countryside may have two. So contraception is widely practiced, especially by couples who already have children.

Usually after giving birth to a child, women are encouraged to have an IUD installed or to be sterilized. For those without either IUDs or sterilization, condoms are used. Condoms used to be given away free, but not now. Usually, each state-owned company in China has a female employee who is in charge of family planning matters. She is supposed to hand out all kinds of contraceptives regularly, mostly condoms, to the employees at the company's expense.

Condoms are also available at drug stores. They are divided into four sizes: large, medium, small, and extra-small. Because some of the Chinese men are too shy to tell the saleswoman what size they want, they resort to the different sizes of coins for help.

When men want a big sized condom, they rotate a five-*fen* coin (approx. the size of a U.S. quarter) on the

counter. The salesperson would get the hint. For a medium, they use a two-*fen* coin (approx. the size of a

U.S. nickel); for a small, a one-*fen* coin (approx. the

size of U.S. dime). I don't know what they use for an extra-small because one-*fen* coin is the smallest, and I don't think people that need an extra-small condom would go there to give themselves away.

+≡— ❋ —≡+

The Chinese have fun with dating expressions. When lovers break up, they usually say

We broke up.
我们吹了.
Wǒ mén chuī le. (*chuī* = to blow)

or

I kicked him (her) off. (I broke up with him or her. I dumped him or her.)
我把他 (她)给蹬了.
Wǒ bǎ tā gěi dēng le.

Chapter 4

EXPLETIVES UNDELETED

1. *Cao*

If you go to China and mingle with young Chinese, you will often hear them spicing their sentences with "fuck" (操 *cào*) here and there. *Cào* is used the same way as "fuck" in English. When it is used as an intransitive verb, it is just the speaker's pet phrase. But this way of speech often gets them in trouble, because *cào* is an offensive word. So if you are a man, don't say it when women are around. If a man uses *cào* in his language to a woman, she would, more often than not, respond:

Keep your mouth clean.
嘴放干净点儿。
Zuǐ fàng gānjìng diǎnr.

or

Have you brushed your teeth (rinsed your mouth) with lavatory water?
你是不是用厕所的水刷过牙(漱过口)?
Nǐ shì bú shì yòng cèsuǒ de shuǐ shuā guò yá (shù guò kǒu)?

Just like in English, a lot of curse terms in Chinese are closely associated with *cào*. For example:

Fuck your mother! (You mother-fucker!)
操你妈 !
Cào nǐ mā!

Fuck your ancestors!
操你祖宗！
Cào nǐ zǔzōng!

Fuck your grandmother!
操你奶奶！
Cào nǐ nǎinai!

Fuck balls! (Shit! or Bullshit!)
操蛋！
Cào dàn!

Fuck your mother's pussy.
操你妈X!*
Cào nǐ mā bī!

These phrases are only used when people get really mad. If men hurl these curse words at each other, usually the quarrel escalates into a brawl.

2. *Zhen ta ma (de)*

"Damn his mother, or Damn it" [真他妈 (的) *zhēn tā mā (de)*] is just as often used as "fuck" (操 *cào*) in informal Chinese conversation. It can be used either to compliment or put down a person or a thing. In most cases, *de* (的) is omitted. When you watch a movie or a TV show and find a woman on screen very

---

*cào was originally written as " 肏 ", which is "enter" (入 *rù*) plus "meat, flesh" (肉 *ròu*), and *bi* written as " 屄 ", which has a recumbent body (尸 *shī*) as radical and cave or orifice (穴 *xué*) as phonetic. It indicates an orifice down there on the body. Because of the pictographic and ideographic nature of the Chinese language, the puritanical Chinese discontinued the use of these two characters. In contemporary Chinese literature, they always use "操" (*cào*) and "X" for that purpose.

beautiful, you can say:

"Oh, what a damn beauty!" ("She's really damn beautiful!")
真他妈 (的)漂亮!
Zhēn tā mā (de) piàoliàng!

to show admiration for her beauty. Or if you see a real muscle man, you could say:

"What a damn great build he has!" ("He got a damn good build!")
真他妈 (的)奘!
Zhēn tā mā (de) zhuǎng!

to indicate admiration and jealousy.

When you want to comment on a sports team that has lost a match badly, you could say:

"What a damned loss!"
输得真他妈 (的)惨！
Shū de zhēn tā mā (de) cǎn!

When you happen upon an ugly person, you could say:

"What a damned ugly face!"
真他妈 (的)丑！
Zhēn tā mā (de) chǒu!

to show the person is extremely ugly. Actually, *zhēn tā mā (de)* can be used before anything. The following points, however, should be noted when using this phrase.

(1) Don't use it to compliment or put down someone that is just by your side or within earshot.

(2) Don't use it on formal occasions.

(3) Don't use it on people with whom you are not familiar, especially women.

(4) You can always use it with your good friends.

Also, *zhēn tā mā de* can be used independently in exactly the same way as the phrase "damn it" in English. In this case *zhēn* rather than *de* can be omitted. For example, if the hard drive gets screwed up when you are working on your computer, you could say:

"Damn it!"
他妈的！
Tā mā de!

Here are more situations in which *zhēn tā mā (de)* is used:

When you come across something that is really gross and makes you very sick, you could say:
真他妈 (的) 恶心！
Zhēn tā mā (de) ě xin! (*ě xin*: sick, disgusting)

When you happen upon a book that is very roughly or crudely written, you could say:
真他妈 (的) 糙！
Zhēn tā mā (de) cāo! (*cāo*: rough, crude)

When you see or hear something that sounds or looks so incredible that you can't believe your eyes, you could say:
真他妈 (的) 绝！
Zhēn tā mā (de) jué! (*jué*: incredible)

When you comment on something that is poorly made, you could say:
真他妈屎！
Zhēn tā mā shǐ! (*shǐ*: shitty)

When you encounter a situation which is very urgent, risky, or dangerous, you could say:

真他妈 (的)要命！

Zhēn tā mā yào mìng! (*yào mìng* literally means "want one's life". Here it can be interpreted as "life-threatening".)

When someone else takes credit that you deserve and you feel cheated, you could say:

真他妈不要脸！

Zhēn tā mā bú yào liǎn! (*bú yào liǎn*: throw away one's face; shameless)

Note: When you are not sure whether or not to use this phrase in a certain situation, don't take the risk. You might embarrass yourself.

3. *Jiba*

Like other languages, Chinese contains a huge number of dirty words related to private parts. Humans are really imaginative. They give private parts so many names you'll never figure out the exact number. The usage of these names is so flexible and varied, it seems they could almost be used anywhere in the language — in a sentence, before a word, in between words — and without any grammar problems! If the words are taken out, it won't affect the meaning of the sentence at all and the sentence will still be grammatically correct. Take "penis" (鸡巴 *jība*) for example, which can be used almost anywhere, just like "fucking" in English. There is a well-known Chinese jingle describing how skinny someone is, which involves the wonderful usage of *jība*:

This *jiba* man (这鸡巴人，*zhè jība rén*)

Is really *jiba* thin (真鸡巴瘦，*zhēn jība shòu*)

Full of *jiba* bones (尽鸡巴骨头，*jìn jība gú tou*)

Without *jiba* flesh. (没鸡巴肉。*méi jība ròu.*)

It seems there is a fad for this way of speaking. Some people like to talk this way, just to show their casualness or nonchalance.

Also, more and more intellectuals, especially of the younger generation, are starting to take a fancy to this kind of street language because they want to be considered more masculine.

Jība is widely used but no one knows why. When you think somebody is talking nonsense, you can say he is "pulling balls" or "pulling genitals". (扯鸡巴蛋 *chě jība dàn*). When people are impervious to reason, or something is jumbled up, you could say that talking to that person or sorting out that thing is as hard as "counting the number of pubic hairs surrounding a penis." (数鸡巴毛 *shǔ jība máo.*) When you find something is mixed up and hard to put back in order, you could say the situation is just like

Penis hairs sautéed with Chinese chives, i.e., it is a mess.

鸡巴毛炒韭菜 – 乱七八糟。

Jība máo chǎo jiǔcài - luàn qī bā zāo.

In colloquial Chinese, *jība* is often used before a word to describe something really bad that has happened or someone who you think is mean.

For example,

> That's really shitty!
> 真鸡巴屎！
> *Zhēn jība shǐ!*

> That jerk!
> 这鸡巴人！
> *Zhè jība rén!*

There are a lot of riddles about *jība* in Chinese. Here is one just for fun:

What is a tree whose bark is peeled upside down, with a pear dangling on each side?
一棵树倒剥皮，一边一个梨。
Yì kē shù dào bā pí, yì biān yí gè lí.

---

4. *Niu bi*

"Ox vagina" (牛 X *niú bī**) is often used by the Chinese, old and young, man and woman, to denote that somebody is blowing the trumpet, bragging or talking his head off, often with an implication of disdain and disgust. Many characters could be used before or after *niú bī* to express the intensity of the speaker's feeling. For example, when you hear that

Note: *Niu bi* can only be used on informal occasions.
* For the usage of "X", please see the section on *cào*, Chapter 4.

somebody has said something that you think is exaggerated, you could say:

Niú bī! 牛X！

Niú bī dà le! 牛X大了！(His or her ox vagina has become so big!)

Niú bī hōng hōng! 牛X烘烘！(His or her ox vagina is steaming!)

Chuī niú bī! 吹牛X！(Blow the ox vagina!)

Chuī niú! 吹牛！(Blow the ox!)

If you hear someone talking about something in high-flown phraseology, for which you have a strong dislike, you could say,

He is blowing the ox vagina so hard. Isn't he afraid that it may explode?
吹牛X也不怕把牛X吹破(炸)了！
Chuī niú bī yě bú pà bǎ niú bī chuī pò (zhà) le!

In some situations, *zhēn niú bī* (真牛X) or *niú bī* (牛X) can be used to express admiration for somebody or something done by somebody.

A: He's got a lucky hand. He wins at every mahjong game.
他的手气很好，每次打麻将都赢。
Tā de shǒuqì hěn hǎo, měi cì dǎ májiàng dōu yíng.

B: That is really marvelous!
真牛X！
Zhēn niú bǐ!

His performance is really brilliant!
他的演出牛X极了！
Tā de yǎnchū niú bī jí le!

5. Taking an oath

The most widely and commonly used oath before the 1980s was

I guarantee or swear in the name of Chairman Mao.
向毛主席保证。
Xiàng máo zhǔxí bǎozhèng.

Chairman Mao Zedong was regarded as a person who always meant what he said and what he said was always deemed correct. After Chairman Mao died in 1976, people gradually discontinued the usage. They began to use other swear words like:

I swear.
我发誓。
Wǒ fāshì.

I swear to the sky.
我对天发誓。
Wǒ duì tiān fāshì.

If I go back on my word, I'll die a lousy death!
如有反悔，不得好死。
Rú yǒu fǎn huǐ, bù dé hǎo sǐ.

If I go back on my word, I'll be executed by heaven and destroyed by earth!
如有反悔，天诛地灭。
Rú yǒu fǎn huǐ, tiān zhū dì miè.

Young lovers often pledge their love to each other by saying,

> The sea may run dry and the rocks may crumble, but our hearts will always remain loyal.
> 海枯石烂不变心。
> *Hǎi kū shí làn bú biàn xīn.*

In daily conversation, people also use the following phrase to emphasize the truthfulness of something.

> What I said is entirely true. If I lied, may I turn into a little dog.
> 我说的全是真的，骗你是小狗。
> *Wǒ shuō de quán shì zhēn de, piàn nǐ shì xiǎo gǒu!*

or

> If I lied to you, I will not be a human being.
> 骗你不是人。
> *Piàn nǐ bú shì rén.*

Some young people would say,

> If I lied, I will be turned into a turtle egg!
> 骗你是王八蛋。
> *Piàn nǐ shì wángbā dàn!* (This is a strong oath.)

Note: *wángbā* (turtle) means a cuckold in Chinese (please see Chapter 1). (Just imagine how bad the egg laid by such a turtle will be!)

6. Quarreling one on one

Beijing is the capital of China. It is a magnet attracting capable people from all over the country. The

educational level of Beijingers is China's highest.
They act nicer to each other than people in other parts
of the country. Even when they are in a quarrel, they
seldom use strong violent words; instead, they resort
to indirect put-downs or insinuations to embarrass
each other or cause each other to be laughed at. But
still there are some young people who really fight.

Beijing is an over-populated city. Transportation is
not easy. Buses are, more often than not, crowded.
Getting on a bus is an ordeal. Only when the people
are literally packed like sardines does the bus begin to
move. This gets even worse in summertime when
people are scantily dressed and the weather is very
hot. Inside the bus the air is a mixture of sweat, per-
fume, body odor, gas... The passengers are like pot
stickers being fried. Under this circumstance it is next
to impossible for people to be in good humor. It is
especially bad at rush hour. When you want to get a
seat on the bus, you have to elbow your way in really
hard. Needless to say, body contact is unavoidable.
Quarrels often break out.

The following is a conversation between two frustrated and angry commuters.

A: "What are you pushing with your snout?! Were
you born in the year of the pig?"
拱什么拱！属猪的呀！
Gǒng shénme gǒng! Shǔ zhū de ya!

B: "What's the point of your barking so loudly?
You must have been born in the year of the dog!"
叫得还真响！你一定是属狗的！
Jiào de hái zhēn xiǎng! Nǐ yídìng shì shǔ gǒu de!

The following fighting conversation usually happens between young men when they bump into each other real hard on the bus:

A: "Fuck your uncle! You are blind in your dog eyes, aren't you?"
操你大爷！瞎了狗眼是不是？
Cào nǐ dà ye! Xiā le gǒu yǎn shì bú shì?

B: "Fuck that scar of your mother's! Who are you cursing?"
你妈那个疤子！你骂谁？
Nǐ mā nà gè bā zi! Nǐ mà shuí?

A: "Mark my words: I am cursing you!"
听清楚了:骂你呢！
Tīng qīngchu le, mà nǐ ne!

B: "Cursing me? I'll punch you, you son-of-a-slave-girl!"
骂我？打你丫挺的！
Mà wǒ? Dǎ nǐ yātíng de!

A: "Wanna fight? I'll keep you company."
想练？我奉陪。
Xiǎng liàn? Wǒ fèng péi.

B: "Let us get off at the next stop and do it."
下站我们下车练。
Xià zhàn wǒ mén xià chē liàn.

7. Talking nonsense

When you hear somebody talking nonsense, there are many ways to show your feeling of disdain.

(1) Fart! (放屁! *fàng pì*)
"Fart" (放屁 *fàng pì*) is used in two ways. It indicates either passing gas or someone's nonsensical talking.

When you smell something weird, you may ask,

"Anybody fart?"
谁放屁了？
Shuí fàng pì le?

When you want to make a confession, you could say,

"I farted."
我放了一个屁。
Wǒ fàng le yí gè pì.

You may also say ,

"He laid a stinking fart."
他放了一个臭屁。
Tā fàng le yí gè chòu pì.

or

"I farted just now. But don't panic. As the saying goes, fart with a sound is odorless; soundless fart stinks."
我放了个屁。但别紧张。臭屁不响，响屁不臭。
Wǒ fàng le gè pì. Dàn bié jǐnzhāng. Chòu pì bù xiǎng, xiǎg pì bú chòu.

Used this way, *le* (了) is often used either at the end of *fàng pì* or inserted in between.

When it is used to indicate "nonsense", *fàng pì* is usually spoken with strong emotions. Both curse words and adjectives can be inserted in between to show emphasis. For example,

Fart!
放屁！
Fàng pì!

Damn fart!
放他妈的屁！
Fàng tā mā de pì!

Stinking fart! (Talk stinking nonsense!)
放臭屁！
Fàng chòu pì!

Sometimes people say,

Dog's fart!
狗屁！or 放狗屁！
Gǒu pì! or Fàng gǒu pì!

What he said is as good as farting!
他说话等于放屁！
Tā shuōhuà děng yú fàng pì!

(2) Sheer nonsense! or Rubbish! (胡说！or 胡说八道！
Hú shuō! or Hú shuō bā dào!)

(3) "Wag one's tongue too freely" or "nonsense" (信口开河 or 信口雌黄 *xìn kǒu kāi hé or xìn kǒu cí huáng*). Both are idioms. The Chinese press often uses this phrase to denounce American government opinions about China.

(4) *Chě dàn* or *Chě jība dàn*

To describe what someone says as sheer nonsense, you can use either "pulling balls" or "pulling genitals" (扯蛋 or 扯鸡巴蛋 *chě dàn* or *chě jība dàn*). For example,

He said that the rooster could lay eggs. That is simply playing the fiddle inside his pants, i.e., pulling genitals!
他说公鸡可以下蛋。 那简直是裤裆里拉胡琴 –
扯鸡巴蛋 !
Tā shuō gōngjī kěyǐ xià dàn. Nà jiǎnzhí shì kùdāng lǐ lā húqín - chě jība dàn!

(5) "Unreasonable talk" or "bullshit" (无稽之谈 *wú jī zhī tán*).

8. Disgusting!

Déxing (德行) is very widely used in Mandarin Chinese. When it is used as an adjective, it means "disgusting" or "shameful". For example,

That guy is really disgusting!
那个家伙真德行 !
Nèige jiāhuo zhēn dé xing!

or

A: "Sorry, I farted."
对不起 , 我放了一个屁。
Duì bù qǐ, wǒ fàng le yí gè pì.

B: "Shame on you."
德行。
Déxing.

When it is used as a noun, for the most part it means anything with bad qualities, such as a disgusting nature and disgusting personality.

For example,

Just have a look at your disgusting personality. How can you be a manager?
瞧你这德行，还想当经理。
Qiáo nǐ zhè déxing, hái xiǎng dāng jīnglǐ.

How can you make a fortune just on the strength of the disgusting nature of your company?
就凭你这公司的德行，还想发财。
Jiù píng nǐ zhè gōngsī de déxing, hái xiǎng fācái.

Chapter 5

FOOD AND DRINK

1. Animal penises and kidneys

For thousands of years the Chinese have used animal penises to cure sexual dysfunction and improve virility. They strongly believe that each animal organ is good for the corresponding part of the human body. For instance, people with chronic gastric disorders are advised to eat animal innards on a frequent basis; sexually weak men should eat animal kidneys and penises.

Conventionally, most Chinese regarded sex only as a way to carry on the family line, as they were raised in a puritanical environment; they didn't know and had no way to know how to enjoy sexual pleasure. In present-day China, as more and more people are exposed to Western ideas, they've begun to give heed to the quality of their sex life. Men in particular are simply obsessed with their virility, and this is responsible for the short supply of varied wines made out of animal penises in the Chinese drug stores.

Dishes made with animal penises are served in many parts of China, catering to the sex-conscious community. Of all the animal penises, the ox penis is most popular and easiest to come by. "Ox penis" (牛鞭) is pronounced *niú biān* (ox whip) in Chinese. Don't order *niú jība* (牛鸡巴) because *jība* is only used on human beings. Do remember the Chinese pronunciation of ox penis; you will find it very useful when you want to try ox penis dishes in China. In many restaurants in Beijing or other cities, dishes prepared with ox penises are served in many different styles. They could be steamed (*qīng zhēng niú biān* 清蒸牛鞭), sautéed (*chǎo niú biān* 炒牛鞭), stewed in brown sauce (*hóng shāo niú biān* 红烧牛鞭), etc. But as long as you know how to say "ox penis" in Chinese, the servers will know exactly what you want. They will show you different ways of cooking it. Don't feel bashful if the servers giggle or laugh, because it means nothing bad. In some restaurants you are allowed to create your own style of penis dishes. Don't be shy to ask. If you like hot spicy food, just go ahead and ask for an ox penis sautéed with chili pepper (*niú biān chǎo là jiāo* 牛鞭炒辣椒), which tastes scrumptious and makes you feel really hot.

Besides animal penises, different styles of dishes cooked with animal kidneys are also available in most Chinese restaurants. "Kidney" (腰子) is pronounced *yāo zi* when referring to an animal organ; it is called *shèn* (肾) when used on human beings. Don't confuse them.

2. More weird food

Some of my friends ask me what animals Chinese don't eat. This is a very tough question, because Chinese seem to eat all kinds of animals — from ants and insects, rats and dogs, to reptiles and scorpions. But after pondering the question over for a while, I find it very easy to answer. Actually, there are a lot of animals Chinese don't eat. For example, Chinese don't eat wolves, because wolves eat human beings. So eating wolf meat is no different from eating human flesh. Chinese never eat small goldfish; when the fish die, they just throw them away. Chinese don't eat mosquitoes or flies, because they are germ-carriers.

If you go to China, however, you will find that restaurants serve a lot of dishes you might have heard of but have never seen before. Snakes, reptiles, dogs, silkworms, and silk cocoons are cooked in different styles and served everywhere. Among these, snakes are the most popular.

In front of many restaurants live snakes are displayed in cages. Just go in and tell the server you want to order a snake dish, and he will take you to the cage and ask you which snake you'd like. After you make the decision, the server will take the snake out, put it on the scales to see how much it weighs (because it is sold by the pound), and kill it either in front of you or in the kitchen, which is up to you. In most cases the snake will be cooked in three styles: snake skin (蛇皮, *shé pí*) sautéed with chili pepper, snake meat (蛇肉, *shé ròu*) brewed in brown sauce, and snake bone soup (蛇汤, *shé tāng*). So if you have ordered a live snake, you don't have to order anything else.

What may surprise you is that before the snake is prepared, the waiter will serve you one glass of red liquor and one glass of white liquor with the snake gallbladder (蛇胆, *shé dǎn*) at the bottom. The liquor is red because it is mixed with the snake blood (蛇血, *shé xiě*), which is said to build up vital energy. In the other glass the gallbladder will be punctured with a toothpick by the server to let out the bile. Stir the liquor and the bile with a chopstick. The white liquor will immediately become green. According to traditional Chinese medicine, the snake gallbladder is good for your eyes. Some people with eye disease even swallow the uncooked snake gallbladder. So don't be scared. The exotic drink on the table will do you no harm.

3. Drying your glass

Chinese are the biggest drinkers in the world.

It seems that everything — from business deals to a personal promotion — can be settled at the dinner table. Not only are they big drinkers, they are also big eaters and wastrels. When they treat friends to dinner at a restaurant they like to show off by ordering more dishes and drinks than necessary. They are in the habit of asking guests to eat this and that throughout the meal to show their hospitality. If you happen to dine with a big drinker, you are doomed. He will compete with you in drinking. He has endless reasons and pretexts to have you drink exactly the same amount of liquor. If you refuse, he might get very mad and take your refusal as a sign of disrespect or disregard for his hospitality. The situation will be even worse if you are in the countryside. The best strategy of escape is to say you are allergic to alcohol at the time you are being invited. You could say,

> Thank you for inviting me. But I cannot drink alcoholic beverages, I am allergic to them.
> 谢谢你邀请我，但我不能喝酒，我酒精过敏。
> *Xièxie nǐ yāoqǐng wǒ, dàn wǒ bù néng hē jiǔ, wǒ jiǔjīng guò mǐn.*

or

> I gave up drinking three years ago. I haven't touched any alcoholic drinks ever since.
> 我戒酒已三年了。这段时间我滴酒未沾。
> *Wǒ jiè jiǔ yǐ sān nián le. Zhè duàn shíjiān wǒ dī jiǔ wèi zhān.*

You can always hear the following toast spoken at a dinner party.

Gān bēi! (干杯!) literally means "dry your glass", or "bottoms up". But in most cases it only means "cheers". When you drink with other guests and touch your glass with somebody else's with an exchange of "*Gān bēi, gān bēi!*", you are advised to sip a little bit and not really dry your glass. If you empty the whole glass, you will be regarded as a big drinker and people at the party would keep treating you to more.

Here are some common expressions used at the dining table:

> Dry one more glass!
> 再干一杯!
> *Zài gān yì bēi!*

Drink to your health!
祝你健康！
Zhù nǐ jiànkāng!

Help yourself to more. Don't stand on ceremony!
多吃点儿。别客气！
Duō chī diǎnr. Bié kèqi!

Help yourself.
自己来。
Zìjǐ lái.

Don't get drunk!
别喝醉了！
Bié hē zuì le!

I don't drink hard liquor. I only drink beer.
我不喝白酒，只喝啤酒。
Wǒ bù hē bái jiǔ, zhǐ hē píjiǔ.

He is drunk.
他醉了。
Tā zuì le.

He is a big drinker. (He can drink a lot.)
他很能喝。
Tā hěn néng hē.

I don't drink alcoholic beverages. Only soft drinks.
我不喝酒，只喝饮料。
Wǒ bù hē jiǔ, zhǐ hē yǐnliào.

I drink only wine, not hard liquor.
我只喝葡萄酒，不喝白酒。
Wǒ zhǐ hē pútao jiǔ, bù hē bái jiǔ.

He is an alcohol ghost (alcoholic).
他是个酒鬼。
Tā shì gè jiǔ guǐ.

I am full. (I am all set.)

我吃饱了。

Wǒ chī bǎo le.

Well known beers in China:

Qingdao Beer: 青岛啤酒 *qīngdǎo píjiǔ*
(Also spelled Tsing Tao)

Wuxing Beer: 五星啤酒 *wǔxīng píjiǔ*
(*wǔxīng* means five stars.)

Beijing Beer: 北京啤酒 *běijīng píjiǔ*

Yanjing Beer: 燕京啤酒 *yànjīng píjiǔ*

Zhujiang Beer: 珠江啤酒 *zhūjiāng píjiǔ*

Well known liquors in China:

Máo Tái 茅台

Fēn Jiǔ 汾酒

Wǔ Liáng Yè 五粮液

Jiàn Nán Chūn: 健南春

Dǒng Jiǔ 董酒

Lú Zhōu Lǎo Jiào 泸州老窖

Jīn Jiǎng Bái Lán Dì 金奖白兰帝
(gold medal brandy)

Zhú Yè Qīng 竹叶青

4. Finger-guessing game

In many parts of China people like to play the "finger-guessing game" (划拳 *huá quán*) at dinner parties. It is a game for two drinking partners to play. Before you get started, your cups must be filled to the rim. The object of the game is to guess the total number of fingers held up by both players. On the count of three, both players call out any number from zero to ten. At the same time each player holds up one hand showing any number of fingers they choose. Whoever says the correct number of the total fingers held up wins. The loser must empty his cup without spilling a drop. After each round the loser's cup is filled again and another round begins. If neither player guesses correctly, then no one drinks and they start over. If both players guess the number correctly, then this is considered a tie and they continue the game. On some occasions spilling a drop carries a penalty of an extra three cups of wine. Sometimes the game is played until one of the players passes out.

Chapter 6

CRIME

1. Prostitution

Prostitution is illegal in China, but it has been there since the very inception of mankind. Especially in present-day China, prostitution permeates almost every nook and corner, in different forms and disguises. Whores in different regions of China accost their targets with different ways of speech. For example, in many cities of Henan province in central China, they would ask,

Do you want to have your pants patched?
你补裤子不补？
Nǐ bǔ kùzi bù bǔ?

They so asked probably because you've got to take off your trousers to have them patched. In other places, they might use other kinds of passwords like "dig a hole" (打洞 *dǎ dòng*), "ignite the dynamite" (点炮 *diǎn pào*), and "eat food" (吃饭 *chī fàn*). Beware!

There are also different prices for different services they perform. For "shoot an airplane" (打飞机 *dǎ fēijī*, a hand-job), the price may be 200 yuan; "beat the waves" (打波 *dǎ bō*) or "eat tofu" (吃豆腐 *chī dòufǔ*), which means fondling breasts or lascivious fumbling, may cost 100 yuan; and the price of "digging a hole" may vary from person to person.

When you are in China, if a strange young woman approaches you and says something you don't quite understand, you'd better not respond. Of course, if you're interested in picking some wild flowers, you may respond nicely and have a chat. But you really should watch out. Many wild flowers are poisonous! And if you are caught by the police, you will face penalties ranging from a exorbitant fine to imprisonment.

If you are a man and check in at a hotel in China (especially in cities in south China), the receptionist might say to you with a smile,

"The weather is cold. Do you need an additional quilt for the night?"
天很冷,晚上需要加褥子吗?
Tiān hěn lěng, wǎnshàng xūyào jiā rùzi ma?

If you say yes, a heavily painted and strongly perfumed woman will knock at your door at night.

Both men and women traveling alone often get sexually harassing phone calls, sometimes in the wee hours of the morning. Most of them are sex invitations. If you are not expecting any long distance calls, the best way to deal with this situation is to take the telephone off the hook.

Prostitution-related words:

prostitute妓女 *jìnǚ*

whore: 娼妓 *chāngjì*

sister of the cave, hooker: 窑姐儿 *yáo jiěr*

girl of the wind and dusts: 风尘女子 *fēngchéng nǚzi*

underground whore, unlicensed prostitute: 暗娼
  àn chāng

loose woman: 荡妇 *dàng fù*

painted woman: 胭脂女 *yānzhi nǔ*

lady of the evening: 夜度娘 *yè dù niáng*

bitch: 婊子 *biǎozi*

chick, whore: 鸡 *jī*

commercial girl, prostitute: 商女 *shāng nǔ*

male hustler: 男妓 *nán jì*

john: 嫖客 *piáo kè*

go-between, pimp: 淫媒 , 皮条客 *yín méi, pí tiáo kè*

madam: 鸨母 , 老鸨 *bǎomǔ, lǎobǎo*

brothel: 妓院 *jì yuàn*

green bowers, brothel: 青楼 *qīng lóu*

chicken-nest, cat-house: 鸡窝 *jī wō*

white-house, brothel: 白房子 *bái fáng zi*

red light district: 花街柳巷 , 红灯区 , 烟花街 *huā jiē liǔ xiàng, hóngdēng qū, yān huā jiē*

prostitution, whoring: 卖淫 *mài yín*

go into prostitution: 从娼 *cóng chāng*

go whoring: 嫖 *piáo*

girl selling spring (youth): 卖春女 *mài chūn nǔ*

girl selling smiles: 卖笑女 *mài xiào nǔ*

selling spring (youth): 卖春 *mài chūn*

sell smiles: 卖笑 *mài xiào*

sell body: 卖身 *mài shēn*

receive a customer: 接客 *jiē kè*

accost: 拉客 *lā kè*

2. Sex offenses

Sex offenders have always been severely dealt with by the Chinese government. Rapists are, more often than not, subject to capital punishment instead of life imprisonment. This contributes to the decrease of sex crimes year after year.

When criminals have been sentenced by a court in China, the court is required to put up posters wherever bills are allowed to be posted, making the criminals and their atrocities known to the public. Usually the poster includes a very detailed account of the criminal's background, how he committed the crime, why he should be sentenced that way, etc. People are interested in reading this kind of poster because they want to learn from the crimes.

The following is a list of words relating to sex offenses.

sex offenses: 性犯罪　*xìng fànzuì*

ravish, rape: 强奸, 奸污　*qiángjiān, jiānwū*

rapist: 强奸犯　*qiángjiān fàn*

He tried to rape me.
他企图强奸我。
Tā qǐtú qiángjiān wǒ.

He raped her savagely.
他粗暴地奸污了她。
Tā cūbào di jiānwū le tā.

In China rapists are usually sentenced to death.
在中国，强奸犯通常被判死刑。
Zài zhōngguó, qiángjiān fàn tōngcháng bèi pàn sǐ xíng.

sexually assault, take liberties with: 猥亵 *wěixiè*

He was sentenced to life imprisonment for sexual assault.
他因猥，妇女而被判终生监禁。
Tā yīn wěixiè fùnǚ ér bèi pàn zhōng shēn jiānjìn.

philander, dally with (women): 顽弄（妇女）*wán nòng (fùnǚ)*

ravish, rape, deflower: 强暴，糟蹋，施暴 *qiáng bào, zāota, shī bào*

She was deflowered at the age of 14.
她十四岁那年被糟蹋了。
Tā shí sì suì nèi nián bèi zāota le.

sodomy: 鸡奸 *jījiān*

sodomite: 鸡奸犯 *jījiān fàn*

seduce: 诱奸 *yòu jiān*

fornication: 通奸 *tōng jiān*

sexual harassment: 性骚扰 *xìng sāorǎo*

He has been sexually harassing me.
他一直对我性骚扰。
Tā yì zhí duì wǒ xìng sāorǎo.

sexual abuse, or sexually abuse: 性虐待 *xìng nüèdài*

3. Pornography

Pornography in any form is outlawed everywhere in China. There is no way to get an X-rated video tape in the normal market, so a lot of deals are made under the table. The dirty tapes keep coming into China from other countries through illegal channels and are circulated and viewed among a myriad of Chinese, both young and old, and men and women. Some of the young people make erotic movies themselves, using some primitive photographic equipment. Of course, if they are caught, they will be jailed.

China has a big market for pornographic tapes (黄色录像 *huángsè lùxiàng*). *Húangsè* literally means "yellow color" which means obscene or pornographic" in Chinese, the equivalent of "blue" in English. Almost all the adult videos available in the United States are also available in China and the only difference is that those in China are of inferior quality, because they are duplicated from duplicates of duplicates of duplicates of the original. So people in China call the X-rated videos "fuzzy movies". (毛片 *máo piān*. *Máo* literally means "hairy". Here it means "unclear".)

The Chinese police have launched many campaigns to fight the spread of "yellow germs", but to no avail. Actually policemen in China enjoy watching those "fuzzy movies" more than anyone else.

4. Bribery

Official corruption has been rampant throughout Chinese history. In present-day China, corruption is so far and wide that even the corrupt Chinese government can't bear it. The government has taken a lot of tough steps, including capital punishment, to curb its spread.

It is well known that Chinese corruption is beyond cure. Nobody can stop it. In China today, to get what you want, you must give first. No bribery, no gain.

It seems that bribery is a must to get anything done. To get a bank loan, a promotion in a company, even permission for marriage, you've got to make a bribe first.

There are many ways to bribe someone. Because making and accepting bribes are both illegal in China, people are very careful. The following is a true story about the process of bribing an official to get the right to mass-produce a product.

Prior to its 45th anniversary, a big bank in China decided to give each of its employees a free gift. Since there were more than 200,000 employees, whoever won the contract to produce the gift would make a fortune. Hearing the news, swarms of individual business people scrambled for the production rights. First they used their connections inside the bank to find out who was the person in control of this project, then devised ways to locate where the man lived. Finally, they began to invent ways to make him say yes.

A friend of mine had been operating a commercial company for several years. He also wanted to make a bid. He and his colleagues discussed many ways to defeat the other companies by buying the project director off. Through their connections in the bank, they found out that the director's birthday was coming up. A plan was made.

They stuffed a doll with thirty thousand yuan (approximately U.S. $3,800) and presented the doll to the project director in person. They told him it was a birthday present and instructed him to be sure that he himself opened and used it.

The next day they gave the director a call and asked him how he liked the gift. He said it was great. So they set up another appointment with him right away. Eventually the deal was made and they produced the anniversary gifts.

As explained previously, making and taking bribes is against the law. People should be very tactful doing it. The most important thing is that you must make the person you've targeted feel he deserves it, is safe and will never get in trouble.

corruption, graft, embezzlement: 贪污 tānwū

public funds: 公款 gōngkuǎn

> He was arrested for embezzling public funds.
> 他因贪污公款而被捕。
> *Tā yīn tānwū gōngkuǎn ér bèi bǔ.*

degeneration, corruption: 腐化 , 腐败 fǔhuà, fǔbài

take bribes: 授贿 , 贪赃 shòu huì, tān zāng

offer (make) a bribe, resort to bribery: 行贿 *xíng huì*

buy over: 收买 , 买通 *shōu mǎi, mǎi tōng*

very demanding, insatiably greedy: 胃口很大, 贪心不足 *wèikǒu hěn dà, tān xīn bù zú* (*wèikǒu* literally means "appetite".)

It is hard to buy him off. He is insatiably demanding.
想买通他不容易 。他胃口太大。
Xiǎng mǎi tōng tā bù róngyì. Tā wèikǒu tài dà.

illicit money: 赃款 *zāng kuǎn*

stolen goods, bribes: 赃物 *zāng wù*

share the booty, share the bribes: 分赃 *fēn zāng*

spend money: 花钱 *huā qián* (spending money implies "to bribe".)

In China today nothing can be done without spending money (resorting to bribery).
当今的中国大陆 ,不花钱办不成事。
Dāng jīn de zhōngguó dà lù, bù huā qián bàn bù chéng shì.

The deal is off

When you want to say a deal is off, the idiomatic way is to use the word "yellow" (黄 *huáng*). For example,

That deal is off.
那笔生意黄了。
Nèi bǐ shéngyì huáng le.

5. Pickpocket

Beware! There are many pickpockets in tourist spots or other public places in big cities like Beijing, Shanghai, Tianjin and Guangzhou. Foreigners look very different from the Chinese and are always targeted by pickpockets. When you have to take an underground train or bus don't put your wallet in the back pocket of your trousers. Be alert because pickpockets sometimes come in groups and they have endless ways to distract you before they make their move. Always place your valuables wherever you think safest.

If you find you have had your pocket picked, you should shout

"Thief!"
有贼！
Yǒu zéi!

"There's a thief!"
有小偷！
Yǒu xiǎotōu!

"My wallet is missing!"
我的钱包不见了！
Wǒ de qiánbāo bú jiàn le!

or

"My pocket is picked!"
我的兜被掏了！
Wǒ de dōur bèi tāo le!
(兜 *dōur*: pouch, pocket; 掏 *tāo*: pick, pickpocket. Both are colloquial and idiomatic words.)

The train or bus attendant might be able to help you. The bus driver may drive all the passengers directly to a police station. The policemen will do what they can to find out who the thief is.

If you happen to catch a pickpocket, it is best to stay quiet for the sake of your safety. You don't know if the thief is alone or has company, so be careful. When you travel in China, keep this in mind, "don't trouble troubles until troubles trouble you."

The most common ways to say "thief" in Chinese:

pickpocket: 小偷, 扒手 *xiǎotōu, páshǒu*

thief: 窃贼, 贼 *qiè zéi, zéi*

three hands: 三只手 *sān zhī shǒu*

6. Narcotics

In the 19th century, many Chinese became addicted to opium imported by Britain. They became so dependent on the drug they couldn't do anything else. Today, as in other countries, drug use is outlawed in China and the government spares no effort to fight drug trafficking.

However, it seems that crime can always find its way anywhere. Drug traffickers can always manage to smuggle all kinds of narcotics into China and the number of drug users there is gradually on the rise. The following are drug-related words:

narcotics: 毒品 *dú pǐn* (*dú* literally means "poison"; *pǐn*, goods or products.)

marijuana: 大麻 *dàmá*

heroin: 海洛因 *hǎiluòyīn*

opium: 鸦片 *yāpiàn*

cocaine: 可卡因 *kěkǎyīn*

LSD: 麻醉剂 *mázuìjì*

morphine: 马啡 *mǎfēi*

drug users, drug addicts: 瘾君子, 大烟鬼 , 吸毒者
   yǐn jūnzǐ, dà yān guǐ, xī dú zhě

drug use, drug-taking: 吸毒 *xī dú*

drug habit, drug addiction: 毒瘾 *dú yǐn*

get high: 吸毒后的快感 *xī dú hòu de kuài gǎn*

deal in drugs, drug trafficking: 贩毒 *fàn dú*

smuggle: 走私 *zǒu sī*

drug dealer, drug trafficker: 毒品贩子, 毒枭 ,
   贩毒者 *dú pǐn fàn zi, dú xiāo, fàn dú zhě*

kick the drug habit: 戒除毒瘾 *jiè chú dú yǐng*

narcotics agents: 缉毒人员 *jí dú rén yuán*

He makes a living by smuggling narcotics.
他以走私毒品为生。
Tā yǐ zǒusī dúpǐn wéi shēng.

To have a drug addict to kick the drug habit is
even harder than to climb up to the sky.
让大烟鬼戒除毒瘾比登天还难。
*Ràng dà yān guǐ jiè chú dú yǐn bǐ dēng tiān hái
nán.*

Dǎ dī in China

When traveling in China, you can always take a taxi to your destination. After you get into the car, simply tell the driver the Chinese name of the place you want to go, and the driver will hit the gas. In most places, cab drivers are honest, and they won't cheat you. Usually when taking a cab around in the daytime in big cities like Beijing and Guangzhou, you should just relax and enjoy the scenery along the way.

But when you just disembark from the plane or take a taxi at night, you might be a target to rip off. Since you are a tourist and you are not very familiar with the geography of the city, you will have no way of knowing where the taxi driver will take you. My suggestion is that you should always pretend to know the city inside and out. Don't disclose your identity as a tourist. Have him mistake you for either a student at a local university or employee with a foreign company. As long as you've read about the city and are prepared in advance, the taxi drivers dare not cheat you.

If you have a tight budget when in Beijing, always try to flag down a "bread-shaped van" (面包车 *miànbāochē*). This kind of taxi is usually yellow in color and the taxi fare is cheap: a maximum charge of 10 yuan in the first ten kilometers. But it is not air-conditioned and in summer it is very hot inside.

"Take a taxi" is 坐(打)出租车 (*zuò (dǎ) chūzūchē*) in Chinese. Now there is a new way to say it. It is *dǎ dī* (打的). For example,

You can either take a bus or a taxi to Zhongshan Park.
去中山公园，你可以坐公共汽车，也可以打的。
Qù zhōngshān gōngyuán, nǐ kéyǐ zuò gōnggòng qìchē, yě kéyǐ dǎ dī.

Chapter 7

TOILETS

1. Public toilets

Public toilets (公厕 *gōng cè*, short for 公共厕所 *gōng gòng cèsuǒ*) can be seen in many places in China. But don't picture them as Western toilets. When you have to use this kind of public toilet, be psychologically prepared, because the strong smell might hit you the moment you step in. Some of them don't even have water to flush. Toilet paper is never provided for free, so don't forget to take toilet paper with you wherever you go in China.

Today there are more and more pay toilets (收费 厕所 *shōu fèi cèsuǒ*). You are supposed to pay 20 cents (in 1993; now the charge might be much more) for admission and a piece of coarse brown-color toilet paper. Even in this kind of toilet, water is not usually supplied for you to wash your hands.

The following is a list of words or phrases relating to toilets.

Men's (Women's) toilet: 男(女)厕所 *nán (nǚ) cèsuǒ*, sometimes shortened to *nán cè* or *nǚ cè*

use the bathroom: 上厕所 *shàng cèsuǒ*

toilet paper: 手纸 *shǒuzhǐ*

smell of urine: 臊 *sāo*

stinking: 臭 *chòu*

urine: 尿 *niào* (*niào* can be used as "to pee" by children.)

feces: 屎 *shǐ*

to defecate: 大便 *dàbiàn* (*Dàbiàn* can also be used as a noun, which means "feces".)

to piss: 撒尿 *sā niào*

to urinate: 小便 *xiǎobiàn* (*Xiǎobiàn* can also be used as a noun, which means "urine".)

shit, crap: 拉屎 *lā shǐ* (*lā shǐ* literally means "pull feces".)

have loose bowels, diarrhea: 拉稀 *lā xī*

wipe the butt: 擦屁股 *cā pìgu*

flush, flush the toilet: 冲水, 冲厕所 *chōng shuǐ, chōng cèsuǒ*)

wash hands: 洗手 *xǐ shǒu*

May I please be excused?
我想方便一下儿。
Wǒ xiǎng fāng biàn yíxiàr.
(This is a very polite way to say "I want to use the bathroom".)

I have to go. I really cannot hold it.
我想拉屎 。我实在憋不住了。
Wǒ xiǎng lā shǐ. Wǒ shízài biē bú zhù le.

Is there a toilet nearby?
附近有厕所吗？
Fùjìn yǒu cèsuǒ ma?

The stinking smell is really unbearable!
气味实在让人受不了！
Qìwèi shízài ràng rén shòu bù liǎo!

The smell is so foul, I can't open my eyes!
臊(臭)得让人睁不开眼睛。
Sāo (chòu) de ràng rén zhēn bù kāi yǎnjīng.

When kids want to tell their mom they want to defecate or urinate, they usually say,

"I want to poop.
我要拉屁屁。
Wǒ yào lā bǎ ba.

I want to pee.
我要尿尿。
Wǒ yào niào niào.

You may say to your child,

"Don't forget to wipe your butt after relieving yourself."
解完大便后不要忘了擦屁股。
Jiě wán dà biàn hòu bú yào wàng le cā pìgu.

"Wiping your ass"

"Wipe ass" (擦屁股 *cā pìgu*) can mean two things. One is the literal act after relieving yourself; the other, to finish something left over by some sloppy person. Example:

You have been an editor for a few decades. How can you let me clean up after you?
都干了几十年的编辑了,还要我给你擦屁股。
Dōu gàn le jǐ shí nián de biānjí le, hái yào wǒ gěi nǐ cā pìgu.

But men must be careful when using this phrase about a woman. Women hate to see or hear "their asses wiped by others". Some men have been ruthlessly embarrassed by women that refuse to have their butts wiped.

2. Toilet literature

China is a puritanical country, at least on the surface. People are still circumspect about sex. A dearth of housing and traditional education make it all the harder for lovers to make love. These suppressed sexual urges are just like a pressure cooker. When the pressure builds enough, it will explode. But how? Of course there are many channels to relieve sexual tension. One of the most commonly seen ways is when people are answering the call of nature. Humans must reproduce, so sex is indispensable; to live, they must eat and relieve themselves, so eating and relieving can also cause pleasure. So when sexually suppressed young people are relieving themselves, many of them simply associate sexual urges with the call of nature by drawing cartoon-style human private parts, vivid sex scenes, or writing dirty poems. If you go to China, chances are you will see them on the walls in all kinds of restrooms.

Toilet literature or 厕所文学 *cèsuǒ wénxué*, was coined by students at Beijing University in the '80s. There was a lot of dirty graffiti on the desks, in toilets, and on campus walls. The university administration was very upset, but couldn't think of any way to stop this. They decided to have all the doors re-white-washed. But as the Chinese saying goes, "the wild fire can never destroy the green grass completely, which will be revived by the spring breeze." So very soon the newly whitewashed doors were scrawled on all over again. This forced the administration officials to think hard for ways to stop the obscenity. An idea finally hit them. They had all the white-painted walls and doors and desks painted black!

China is undergoing an economic reform and is importing all kinds of things from western countries. Maybe they should also import western ways to stop the spread of toilet literature. In some U.S. universities, the administration places chalk boards on each door of the bathroom. Students can use chalk to write or draw whatever is on their minds. This is much easier to wipe out. If this is adopted by Chinese universities, they can save a lot of money by not repainting. But whether the Chinese students like their works to be wiped out so easily, I am not sure!

Chapter 8

JUDGING PEOPLE

1. Dumb as a wooden chicken

The Chinese always think of themselves as the best. As a result, they are in the habit of looking down upon each other. When a Chinese person is alone, he or she is very hard to defeat; but when many Chinese get together for a task, they usually fall apart before it is completed. They all think differently, regard themselves as VIPs, and go in different directions.

This national characteristic might account for the large number of put-downs in the language. When they put down somebody or something, they think words like "foolish or stupid" are not enough; they often follow those words with female or male genitals. They often use "stupid cunt" (傻X *shǎ bī*) to curse a female and "stupid dick" (傻鸡巴 *shǎ jība*) to curse a male. Moreover, they often use "stupid cunt" and "stupid dick" interchangeably, i.e., they use "stupid dick" for a woman and "stupid cunt" for a man.

Now some people prefer *shǎ bō ī* (傻波依) to *shǎ bī*, to avoid the offensive sound of the pronunciation of *bī*. Actually they have the same meaning, as the *pinyin* romanization of *bī* is made up of *b* (pronounced *bō* in *pinyin*) and *ī*.

To go to extremes, they might add "fucked by a slave girl" (丫挺的 *yā tǐng de*) to *shǎ bī* — namely, *shǎ bī yā tǐng de*, meaning, somebody "comes into this world through the stupid cunt of a slave girl."

Of course, there are a lot of other words or phrases to depict a stupid or a slow person. Please see the following list.

stupid person: 二百五 *èr bǎi wǔ* (literally means two hundred fifty)

stupid, foolish: 愚蠢 *yú chǔn* (used on both formal and informal occasions)

wooden-headed, dull-witted: 木 *mù* (literally meaning wood or tree. Informal, often used by Beijingers)

slow-witted, dull: 呆 *dāi* or 呆头呆脑 *dāi tóu dāi nǎo* (colloquial, used in most places in China)

foolish-looking, muddle-headed: 傻头傻脑 *shǎ tóu shǎ nǎo*

slow and blunt: 迟钝 *chí dùn*

mentally retarded, dementia: 痴呆 *chī dāi*

slow, clumsy, dull: 笨 *bèn* (colloquial)

dumb as a wooden chicken: 呆若木鸡 *dāi ruò mù jī*

How come you are so slow?
你怎么那么木？
Nǐ zěnme nàme mù?

How can a slow person like you learn to drive?
呆头呆脑的，怎么学车？
Dāi tóu dāi nǎo de, zěnme xué chē?

stupid egg: 笨蛋 *bèn dàn* (colloquial)

person of low IQ: 低能儿 *dī néng ér*

stupid melon, blockhead: 傻瓜 *shǎ guā* (colloquial)

person of low intelligence: 弱智 *ruò zhì*

stupid product: 蠢货 *chǔn huò*

fool: 傻子 *shǎzi*

weak-minded person, a fool: 阿斗 *ā dǒu* (the infant name of Liu Shan, last emperor of Shu Han (221-263), known for his want of ability and weakness of character)

fool, a silly person: 傻冒 *shǎ mào* (which has been used in Beijing for many years and is still being used.)

If you are a white person, you are called either *bái rén* (白人) or *bái zhǒng rén* (白种人) in Chinese. There is no difference between the two. If you are a black person, you are almost always called *hēi rén* (黑人), and seldomly called *hēi zhǒng rén* 黑种人. If you are a yellow person, you are always called *huáng zhǒng rén* (黄种人) and never *huáng rén* (黄人). Only God knows why.

And if you are of mixed blood, you are a *hùn xuě ér* (混血儿). It is believed in China people of mixed blood are smarter.

Other nicknames for white people are "foreign devils" (洋鬼子 *yáng guǐzi*), "big nose" (大鼻子 *dà bízi*), "long nose" (长鼻子 *cháng bízi*). A derogatory name for blacks is "black devils" (黑鬼 *hēi guǐ*).

2. Skinny and fat

Most Chinese are skinny (瘦 *shòu*), partly because of hereditary factors, partly because of their diet. Although there are plenty of skinny people in China, being skinny is not deemed something commendable. Instead, the language abounds with derogatory words to put down thin people, and a skinny person is often compared to a monkey or ghost. For example, the Chinese often use phrases like

thin and emaciated like a stick: 骨瘦如柴 *gǔ shòu rú chái*

a bag of bones: 一把骨头 *yì bǎ gútou*

bones wrapped up in skin, only skin and bone: 皮包骨头 *pí bāo gútou*

sesame stalk, drain pipe: 麻干儿 *má gǎnr*

bean sprout: 豆芽菜 *dòuyá cài* (often used to describe a tall thin person)

likely to fall when a current of wind blows: 风一吹就倒 *fēng yì chuī jiù dǎo*

as thin as a ghost: 瘦得象鬼 *shòu de xiàng guǐ*

a skinny monkey: 瘦猴 *shòu hóu*

a skinny person: 瘦子 *shòu zi*

For thousands of years, the Chinese have regarded being fat (胖 *pàng*) as a sign of good health. In modern times, science has proved that people don't have to be fat to be healthy. There are a lot of put-down words for being fat, and fat is often associated with pigs and sometimes with laziness. For example,

a whole body of flesh: 一身肉 *yì shēn ròu*

a whole body of fat: 一身膘 *yì shēn biāo* (*biāo* is used to describe an plump and sturdy animal, so when it is used on a human, it is derogatory.)

as fat as a pig: 胖得象猪似的 *pàng de xiàng zhū sì de*

as fat as a pig, big-bellied: 大腹便便 *dà fù piánpián*

fat: 肥 *féi* (*féi* is usually used to refer to animals; so when used on a man, it is derogatory.)

When you want to say in Chinese "someone is fat" and don't want to offend him or her, you should say *tā hěn pàng* (他很胖) rather than *tā hěn féi* (他很肥).

The Chinese are in the habit of putting down others to elevate themselves. They put down skinny and fat people to show they themselves are just shaped right — neither fat nor skinny.

Wearing a green hat

To "Wear a green hat" (戴绿帽子 *dài lǜ màozi*) refers to a man whose wife is having an extramarital affair. It is said that during the Ming dynasty, the law stipulated that those men who had unfaithful wives and who also worked in brothels must wear a green hat. Since then, a cuckold has been referred to as a man wearing a green hat.

3. Rich and poor

"The poorer, the more glorious." People in China used to feel very proud of being poor (穷 *qióng*). When the People's Republic of China was founded, being rich (富 *fù*) was something to be ashamed of. The rich were deprived of their wealth, were demonstrated against, humiliated in the streets and made to wear high cylinder-shaped hats. Only in the 1980s did people begin to look up to those who had money and knew how to make money. Poverty became the last thing to be proud of. Now their perspective on money has entirely changed. The poor are looked down upon and the rich are highly regarded. People are simply desperate for money. They all try to "catch up with the Joneses." Nobody wants to be left behind.

The economic reform has produced many rich people in China, resulting in some new terms to describe them, such as "big money" (大款 *dà kuǎn*, or 大亨 *dà hēng*) and "grandfather of money" (款爷 *kuǎn yé*). The most common ways of referring to the rich are "man of wealth" (富翁 *fù wēng*), "man with money" (有钱人 *yǒu qián rén*) and "rich and powerful person" (富豪 *fù háo*).

The Chinese language abounds with terms and phrases describing poverty. Please see the following list of words and phrases, all of which are mostly used in daily conversation.

poor, poverty-stricken: 穷 *qióng*
poor person: 穷人 *qióng rén*

pauper, poor wretch: 穷光蛋 *qióng guāng dàn*

pauper: 穷棒子 *qióng bàng zi*

so poor that he cannot even afford a stick to beat the drum but has to use his penis for the job: 穷得鸡巴打鼓 *qióng de jība dǎ gǔ*

so poor that he (she) doesn't have enough trousers to cover himself or herself: 穷得没有裤子穿 *qióng de méiyǒu kùzi chuān*

poor and pedantic: 穷酸 *qióng suān*

broke, lack of money: 缺钱 *quē qián*

so poor that he has only coins (no paper money) clicking (clattering) in his pocket: 穷得叮当响 *qióng de dīng dāng xiǎng* (*dīng dāng* means a click or clatter.)

Cream or Cream Cakes

"Cream" (奶油 *nǎiyóu*) or "cream cake" (奶油蛋糕 *nǎiyóu dàngāo*) is often used colloquially to describe a man who is very handsome with ladylike features. His complexion is white and creamy and he may not have a conspicuous beard or mustache. Many young women in China have a crush on this type of man. The connotation is derogatory.

Most of the male Chinese movie stars look more like women.
中国的电影名星大部分都很奶油。
Zhōngguó de diànyǐng míngxīng dà bù fèn dōu hěn nǎiyóu.

or

中国的电影名星大部分都是奶油蛋糕。
Zhōngguó de diànyǐng míngxīng dà bù fèn dōu shì nǎiyóu dàngāo.
(Note: *nǎiyóu* is used as an adjective and *nǎiyóu dàngāo* as a noun.)

4. Eating vinegar

You may happen upon many situations when you want to vent your jealousy or comment upon somebody that is prone to jealousy. When Chinese want to say somebody is jealous, they often say he likes "eating vinegar" (吃醋 *chī cù*).
For example,

Don't talk to Xiao Wang. His wife may get jealous.
别跟小王说话, 他老婆爱吃醋。
Bié gēn xiǎo wáng shuō huà, tā lǎopo ài chī cù.

There are many other ways to show jealousy or talk about jealousy in Chinese. The following words are often used.

envy, jealousy: 忌妒, 妒忌 *jì du, dù ji*
consumed with envy: 妒火中烧 *dù huǒ zhōng shāo*

Seeing her boy friend fall in love with another woman, she feels consumed with jealousy.
看到她的男朋友爱上了别的女人, 她妒火中烧。
Kàn dào tā de nán péngyǒu ài shàng le bié de nǚ rén, tā dù huǒ zhōng shāo.

sour grapes: 吃不着葡萄说葡萄酸 *chī bù zháo pútao shuō pútao suān*

He said Xiao Wang's wife looks ugly. This is actually nothing but sour grapes.
他说小王的夫人长得难看, 这不过是吃不着葡萄说葡萄酸。
Tā shuō xiǎo wáng de fūrén zhǎng de nán kàn. zhè bú guò shì chī bù zháo pútao shuō pútao suān.

Americans use "green eyes" for jealousy while Chinese use "red eyes" or "red eye disease" (红眼 *hóng yǎn* or 红眼病 *hóng yǎn bìng*). For example,

> Seeing that other people have made a fortune, he feels very envious.
> 看到别人发财，他的眼红了。
> *Kàn dào bié ré fā cái, tā de yǎn hōng le.*

Do you know?

Policemen are often called "dog" (狗子 *gǒuzi*). This term was originally used by social misfits. Now some young people use it to show dislike for policemen.

Police stations or jails are nicknamed *jú zi* (局子). You could say,

> He has been jailed three times.
> 他进了三次局子。
> *Tā jìn le sān cì jú zi.*

Shooting the breeze

"Chop the big mountain" (砍大山 *kǎn dà shān*) means exactly the same as the English phrase "shoot the breeze".

> Every day he does nothing but shoot the breeze.
> 每天除了砍大山以外他什么都不干。
> *Měi tiān chú le kǎn dà shān yǐ wàn, tā shěnme dōu bú gàn.*

Chapter 9

FALLING ILL

1. Be careful about what you eat

The last thing you want when you travel in China is to get sick, because it would screw up your whole vacation. But you never know when and how the illness may intrude on your system, since you are exposed to an environment populated by germs totally foreign to you.

(1) In some parts of China night soil (human waste) (大粪 dà fèn) is still being used to accelerate the growth of vegetables. Never eat raw vegetables in China.

(2) Don't drink tap water before it is boiled, because it contains more bacteria than your immune system can kill.

(3) To keep insects away from fruit, more insecticide than allowed is sprayed. You shouldn't eat fruit such as apples, pears and dates without first removing the skin. If you love fruit, you should make sure to peel it first.

2. Going to the doctor

Pollution is worsening in big cities in China, causing many tourists to contract respiratory diseases. Flu is very common. Don't forget to take medicines (aspirin, etc.) with you on your trip. In case you need to see a doctor, you should contact the information desk of your hotel. If possible, bring a translator with you. If you have to get a shot, be sure to tell the nurse you want to use disposable syringes (一次性使用注射器 *yícì xìng shīyòng zhùshè qì*), and the nurse will let you know how to get them.

The following is a list of medical terms you should know:

flu: 流感 *liúgǎn*

the common cold: 感冒 *gǎnmào*

have a fever, run a temperature: 发烧 *fāshāo*

headache: 头痛 *tóu tòng*

dizziness: 头晕 *tóu yūn*

stomachache: 肚子痛 , 腹痛 *dùzi tòng, fù tòng*

sore throat: 嗓子痛 *sǎngzi tòng*

fatigue: 疲倦 *pí juàn*

nausea: 恶心 *ě xīn*

vomiting: 呕吐 *ǒu tù*

cough: 咳嗽 *késou*

diarrhea, loose bowels: 拉肚子 , 腹泻 *lā dùzi, fù xiè*

toothache: 牙疼 *yá téng*

dysentery: 痢疾 *lìji*

constipation: 便秘 *biàn bì*

pneumonia: 肺炎 *fèiyán*

mental depression: 精神抑郁症 *jīngshén yìyù zhèng*

menstrual pain: 经痛，月经痛 *jīng tòng, yuèjīng tòng*

hemorrhoid: 痔疮 *zhìchuāng*

chest pain: 心绞痛 *xīn jiǎo tòng*

lumbago: 腰痛 *yāo tòng*

ankle sprain: 踝关节扭伤 *huái guānjié niǔ shāng*

food poison: 食物中毒 *shíwù zhòng dú*

insomnia: 失眠 *shī mián*

venereal disease: 性病，花柳病 *xìng bìng, huā liǔ bìng*

syphilis: 梅毒 *méidú* (*méidú* literally means plum poison.)

gonorrhea: 淋病 *lìnbìng*

herpes: 疱疹 *pàozhěn*

AIDS: 爱滋病 *àizībìng*

Chest Pain

A female tourist went to a doctor in China for chest pain. The doctor asked her, "What's wrong with you?"

"I am suffering from chest pain," she answered.

"You need an examination," the doctor said and then asked her to lie down on the examining bed and told her to take off her pants. The woman was very surprised to hear that and asked the doctor why she had to take off her pants. The doctor said, " Since you feel pain during sex, of course you need a check-up. Don't panic. I'll have a woman doctor examine you."

The woman flushed red. She now realized that there must be something wrong with her pronunciation of "chest pain" in Chinese. So she pointed at her left chest and told the doctor that she had pain right there. Finally the doctor got it. What the patient meant to say was "chest pain" (心绞痛 xīn jiǎo tòng) rather than "pain during sexual intercourse" (性交痛 xìngjiāo tòng).

Chapter 10

WEDDINGS AND FUNERALS

Weddings and funerals are known as *hóng bái xǐ shì* 红白喜事. "Red" (红 *hóng*) indicates weddings, "white" (白 *bái*), funerals, and *xǐ shì* (喜事), happy occasions. The death of a friend or relative, especially an old person, is of course a matter of grievance, but according to some Chinese, death, viewed from another perspective, is a blessing for the person because he or she has left this wicked world for a happy afterlife. That's why I put weddings and funerals together in the same chapter.

1. Gift-giving at the wedding

If you are invited to attend a Chinese wedding, you should bring a gift along. The gift may be cash (or a check) placed in a red envelope inserted in between the wedding card, bed spread, blanket, pressure cooker, etc. But remember: don't buy a clock as a wedding gift. "Clock" is pronounced *zhōng* (钟) in Chinese, which is homonymous with *zhōng* (终), meaning end or death. So "presenting a clock" (送钟 *sòng zhōng*) sounds like "attending upon a dying person" (送终 *sòngzhōng*).

In many places of China, people present peanuts (花生 *huāshēng*) to newlyweds, because *huā* means "many or prolific" and *shēng*, birth. So to give peanuts is to wish the couple to have as many children as they want. This is in accord with the traditional Chinese concept of "more children, more happiness."

The following sentences are often used when presenting the gift to the newlyweds:

Congratulations! May you remain a devoted couple forever!
恭喜，恭喜！愿你们白头偕老！
Gōngxǐ, gōngxǐ! Yuàn nǐmen bái tóu xié lǎo!

This little gift is intended to show my wishes for your eternal happiness.
这只是一点儿心意。祝你们永远幸福。
Zhè zhǐ shì yìdiǎnr xīnyì. Zhù nǐmen yǒngyuǎn xìngfú.

I hope you will give birth to precious children as soon as possible.
盼你们早生贵子。
Pàn nǐmen zǎo shēng guì zǐ.

2. Offering condolences

There are many ways to say "to die" or "death" in Chinese, but it is not easy to use them correctly at the appropriate time. The principle is that when you are not sure which word you should use, just use "die" (死 *sǐ*) under all circumstances. Although it may sound out of place in some cases, at least you won't be laughed at or offend the relatives.

When you offer your condolences to the family members and relatives of a dead person, you are advised to use the following sentences as references.

1. ... has left us. I feel very sorry. But a dead person cannot come back to life. So you shouldn't grieve too much.

…走了,我很难过。但人死了不能复生 。你一定要节哀。

… zǒule, wǒ hěn nánguò. Dàn rén sǐ le bù néng fù shēng. Nǐ yí dìng yào jié āi.

(When you offer condolences, try to use "has left" (离开了 *líkāile*) or "has gone" (走了 *zǒule*) instead of the word "die" (死 *sǐ*).

2. Don't be too sad. You should do your best to control yourself and take care of yourself.

要节哀。要尽量控制自己 ,保重自己的身体。

Yào jié āi. Yào jìnliàng kòngzhì zìjǐ, bǎozhòng zìjǐ de shēntǐ.

No matter how you are going to say it, don't forget to use *jié āi* (节哀). *Jié āi* literally means "save grief".

Ways to say "die" in Chinese:

to die: 死 *sǐ* (used almost on all occasions)

sacrifice one's life, give one's life to: 捐躯 ,牺牲 ,献身 *juān qū, xī shēng, xiàn shēn* (used when somebody died for a cause or a country)

pass away: 去世 *qùshì* (euphemism for *sǐ*. Used the same way as "pass away" in English.)

驾崩 *jiàbēng*. *Jià* means an emperor's cart, implying the emperor himself; *bēng*, the death of an emperor. In ancient China, when an emperor died, people couldn't use *sǐ*. They must say the emperor "*jiàbēng le*." (In China today, people are still using it for comic effect.)

pass away: 逝世 *shìshì* (used on formal occasions)

gone to see Marx: 见马克思去了 *jiàn mǎkèsī qù le*. (used on informal occasions. Sometimes used for fun.)

has left this world: 离开了这个世界 *líkāi le zhègè shìjiè*

has gone to see God: 见上帝 *jiàn shàngdì*

die a natural death: 寿终 *shòuzhōng* (literally means "long life ended". Used only for old men who died of old age at a good time and good place.)

go to see Confucius: 去见孔夫子 *qù jiàn kǒngfūzǐ*

⊷ ✳ ⊶

Where, where

A foreigner attended a Chinese wedding. He went up to the bride and groom and said to the bride very politely, "You are really beautiful." The groom said to him, "*Nǎli, nǎli.*" (哪里，哪里。) *Nǎli* literally means "where, where". Unfortunately, the foreigner didn't know "*nǎli, nǎli*" used here was a self-depreciatory expression and meant "it is nothing". He was very surprised by the groom's response, thinking that praising by generalization was not enough for this Chinese guy and that he should go on praising the bride more specifically. So he said in very stiff Chinese, "Her hair, eyes, nose, ears, neck and brows are all beautiful." This set all the people there laughing until their sides burst.

Chapter 11

IDIOMS TO WATCH OUT FOR

Chinese characters could be pronounced according to the pronunciation of part of the character; even if you mispronounce it, it won't be too serious a mistake.

中国字念半边，错也不会错上天。

Zhōngguó zì niàn bàn biān, cuò yě bú huì cuò shàng tiān.

This jingle about Chinese pronunciation rules has led to a myriad of pronunciation mistakes and jokes, since many people believe it.

Idioms are frequently used in Chinese conversations. But many Chinese, including teachers and professors, have been ridiculed for mispronouncing a certain character in an idiom. As is well known, the pronunciation of Chinese characters is much harder than that of English words, because there are no rules to go by. You have to simply remember the pronunciation of characters one by one. The pronunciation mistakes people make are partly attributed to their laziness and unwillingness to consult a dictionary, and partly to their belief in the above-mentioned jingle.

Once a professor at Beijing University was lecturing on Music History. While he was telling a story about an ancient European king, he said,

"This king was opinionated."

这个国王刚愎自用。

Zhège guówáng gāng fù zì yòng.

At this the whole class began to laugh. The professor looked very confused at first, then he laughed very proudly, probably thinking he had used a good idiom that had a tremendous effect on the students. What actually set the class laughing was that he mispronounced the character 愎 *bì* , which is a mistake commonly made by the Chinese. 愎 is often mispronounced *fù*, because 复 on the right side of the character is pronounced *fù*. The tragedy is that the professor himself didn't realize his mistake. Even after more than ten years passed, my classmates and I could still remember the mistake made by this professor, because that kind of mistake was not supposed to be made by a well-educated person.

Students learning Chinese should really pay attention to the tricky pronunciation of some characters in Chinese, especially in idioms. Don't even try to guess the pronunciation of a character you have never seen before. Always consult a dictionary for the correct pronunciation to avoid embarrassment.

The following list includes the most typical pronunciation mistakes made by the Chinese when they are using idioms in their speech.

乳臭未干 *rǔ xiù wèi gān* (be wet behind the ears). The character 臭 can be pronounced either *chòu* or *xiù*. In this idiom, it is read as *xiù*.

冗词赘句 *rǒng cí zhuì jù* (verbose, wordy). Don't confuse *rǒng* 冗 with *chén* 沉.

千里迢迢 *qiān lǐ tiáo tiáo* (over a great distance). Don't confuse *tiáo* 迢 with *zhāo* 招.

劈荆斩棘 *pī jīng zhǎn jí* (make one's way through the jungle and bushes). Don't confuse *jí* 棘 with *cì* 刺.

惘然若失 *wǎng rán ruò shī* (wear a blank look). Don't confuse *wǎng* 惘 with *máng* 茫.

如火如荼 *rú huǒ rú tú* (like raging fire). Don't confuse *tú* 荼 with *chá* 茶 (tea). They look so much alike.

病入膏肓 *bìng rù gāo huāng* (The disease has attacked the vitals - beyond cure). Don't confuse *huāng* 肓 with *máng* 盲 (blind).

恬不知耻 *tián bù zhī chǐ* (shameless). Don't mistake *tián* 恬 for *guā* 括.

温情脉脉 *wēn qíng mò mò* (full of tender feeling). The character 脉 can be pronounced either *mò* or *mài*. Usually this character is read as *mò* when it refers to tender emotions, and as *mài* when referring to the pulse or vein.

言简意赅 *yán jiǎn yì gāi* (concise and comprehensive). Don't mistake *gāi* 赅 for *hài* 骇.

相形见绌 *xiāng xíng jiàn chù* (pale by comparison; be outshone). Don't confuse *chù* 绌 with *zhuō* 拙.

刎颈之交 *wěn jǐng zhī jiāo* (bosom friends who are willing to die for one another). Don't mispronounce *wen* 刎 as *wù* 勿.

自给自足 *zì jǐ zì zú* (able to support oneself; self sufficiency). The character 给 is usually pronounced *gěi*, meaning "to give, provide". But in this idiom it is read as *jǐ*.

置若罔闻 *zhì ruò wǎng wén* (turn a deaf ear to). Don't confuse *wǎng* 罔 with *máng* 茫.

有恃无恐 *yǒu shì wú kǒng* (secure in the knowledge that one has strong backing). Don't confuse *shì* 恃 with *chí* 持.

脍炙人口 *kuài zhì rén kǒu* (win universal praise). Don't mispronounce *kuài* 脍 as *huì* 绘.

一鼻孔出气 *yī bíkǒng chū qì* (breathe through the same nostrils; sing the same tune; gang up with). Be careful with the pronunciation of 鼻 *bí* and pay attention to its tone mark. Don't read it in the first tone as *bī*. (See Chapter 1)

大腹便便 *dà fù pián pián* (as fat as butter). Don't mispronounce 便 here as *biàn*.

阿谀逢迎 *ē yú féng yíng* (curry favor with). Don't read the character 阿 here as *ā*.

好逸恶劳 *hào yì wù láo* (love ease and hate work; hanker after living in comfort and hates labor). Don't read 恶 here as *è*. The character 恶 is pronounced *è* when it refers to "evil" or "ferocious", and *wù* when it is used to indicate "hate" or "dislike".

自认晦气 *zì rèn huì qì* (admit defeat in good grace). Don't mistake *huì* 晦 for *méi* 霉.

不屑一顾 *bú xiè yí gù* (not worth taking a look at). Don't confuse *xiè* 屑 with *xiāo* 肖.

草菅人命 *cǎo jiān rén mìng* (treat human life as no more than grass; have complete disregard for human life). Don't mistake *jiān* 菅 for *guǎn* 管.

参差不齐 *cēn cī bù qí* (uneven, not uniform). Don't read 参差 here as *cān chā*.

馋涎欲滴 *chán xián yù dī* (mouth drooling with greed, keep one's covetous eye). Don't confuse *xián* 涎 (saliva) with *yán* 延.

瞠目结舌 *chēng mù jié shé* (stare tongue-tied; stunned and speechless). Don't confuse the character 瞠 with *táng* 堂. This is a mistake commonly made by native Chinese speakers.

绰绰有余 *chuò chuò yǒu yú* (more than enough to meet the need). Don't mistake *chuò* 绰 for *zhuō* 卓.

Appendix A

CHINESE PHONETIC GUIDE

1. Pronunciation Guide for Chinese in Both *Pinyin* and Wade-Giles

(All English phonemes according to standard US. English)

Pinyin	Wade-Giles	Equivalent English Phoneme
a	a	"o" as in "dot"
b	p	"b" as in "big"
c	ts	"ts" as in "hats"
d	t	"d" as in "radar"
e	er	no English phoneme; "oe" as in French "oevre"
f	f	"f" as in "feather"
g	k	"g" as in "god"
h	h	"h" as in "hot"
i (before n)	i or ih	"i" as in "pin"
i (after sh)	ih	"ur" as in "purr"
i (after other consonants)	i or ee	"ee" as in "sweet"
j	ch	"j" as in "jar"
k	k'	"k" as in "kite"
l	l	"l" as in "limp"
m	m	"m" as in "moan"
n	n	"n" as in "nut"

o	aw	"o" as in "frog"
p	p'	"p" as in "pig"
q	ch'	"ch" as in "chest"
r	j	"j" as in "jug"

(Chinese has a second "r"-like sound as well with no
equivalent English phoneme)

s	s	"s" as in "sex"
t	t'	"t" as in "toy"
u	eu	"oo" as in "moon"
w	w	"w" as in "wand"
x	hs	"sh" as in "she"
y	io	"y" as in "young"
z	tz	"dz" as in "words"
ai	i	"y" as in "buy"
ao	au	"ou" as in "proud"
ei	ay or ai	"ay" as in "lay"
ia	ya or ia	"ya" as in "yard"
iao	yao or iao	"eow" as in "meow"
iu	iu	"yo" as in "yo-yo"
ui	uay or uai	"way" as in "sway"
uo	aw	"aw" as in "saw"
ng	ng	"ng" as in "hang"
sh	shr	"shr" as in "shrimp"
zh	dz, tz, or dh	no equivalent pho-neme; halfway between "dr" as in "drop" and "dz" as in "words"

2. Tones

The Chinese language has different tones that are capable of differentiating meanings. Differences in tone convey different meanings to otherwise identical or similar syllables. In the Beijing dialect, which Mandarin Chinese is based on, there are four basic tones, which are written as follows, using the syllable "*ba*" as an example:

First tone: represented by the tone-graph " ˉ ", a high, level pitch. *bā* (八 in this tone can mean the number 8.

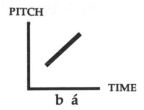

Second tone: represented by the tone-graph " ˊ ", it is a rising tone, starting about mid-range of a speaker's voice, and ending slightly above the first tone. *bá* (拔) can mean "to uproot".

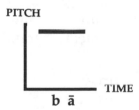

Third tone: represented by the tone-graph " ˇ ", it is a dipping pitch, falling from mid-range to low, then rising. *bǎ* (把) can mean "to hold".

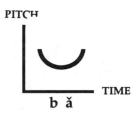

Fourth tone: represented by the tone-graph " ˋ ", it is a sharply falling pitch, starting near the top of the speaker's range and reaching mid- to low-level at the end. *bà* (霸) can mean "tyrant" or "despot".

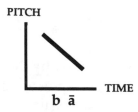

Besides, brief, unstressed syllables may also occur and take a feeble tone, such as *ba* (吧). They have no tone mark.

Appendix B

INDEX OF ENGLISH TERMS

A

AIDS 97
alcohol ghost (alcoholic) 61, 62
anal sex 36
anus 33, 34
aphrodisiac 36
as fat as a pig 89
as thin as a ghost 88
attending upon a dying person 99

B

bad breath 34
bad luck 31
bag of bones 88
balls 33, 46, 55
big money 90
big nose 87
bitch 67
black devils 87
blow the ox vagina 48
bottoms up 61
bribery 71, 73
brothel 67
bullshit 42, 55
butt eye 34
buttocks 33
buy and sell 6

C

cannot hold it 80
Chairman Mao 23, 49
cheers 61
chick 4, 5, 67

D

dumped 39

E

eat tofu 65
eating vinegar 92
ecstasy 35
ejaculate 31, 35
embezzlement 72
envy 16, 92
executed by heaven and destroyed by earth 49

F

fail to lift it up 35
fart 53, 54, 55
feces 80
finger-guessing game 64
first wedding night 28, 29
flesh 10, 42, 46, 89
flush the toilet 80
fool 87
foreign devils 87
foreskin 7, 32
French kiss 34
frigid 36
fuck 27, 46
fuck balls 42
fuzzy movie 70

G

get drunk 62
get wet 34
go back on my word 49
go to bed 27, 28
go whoring 67
gonorrhea 97

thigh 33
three hands 75
tits 33
toilet literature 82, 83
toy 33
turtle 5, 50
turtle egg 50
turtle head 32
twelve o'clock 37
two hundred fifty 86

U

urinate 80, 81

V

vagina 2, 33
virgin 36

W

whore 66, 67
wife 20, 21, 25
wipe the butt 80

Y

yellow 70, 73, 77, 87

Bibliography

Chu, Valentin. *Yin Yang Butterfly: Ancient Chinese Sexual Secrets for Western Lovers*. New York: Tarcher/Putnam, 1993.
Well-done modern survey of ancient Chinese sex techniques.

Constantine, Peter. *Japanese Street Slang*. New York: Tengu Books, 1993.

Humana, Charles & Wang, Wu. *Chinese Sex Secrets - A Look behind the Screen*. Hong Kong: CFW Publications Limited, 1984.

Ishihara, Akira & Levy, Howard S. *The Tao of Sex*. Yokohama: Shibundo, 1969.

Liu, Xun et al. *Practical Chinese Reader (Book 1)*. Beijing: Commercial Press, 1993.

Van Gulik, R. H. *Erotic Color Prints of the Ming Period*. Private Edition.
Hard-to-find book, available through the Oriental Bookstore in Pasadena, California.

Van Gulik, R. H. *Sexual Life in Ancient China*. E. J. Brill, 1961
Classic survey by the famous sinologist and Judge Dee mystery writer. Available in a reprinted edition through the Oriental Bookstore in Pasadena, California.

Wang, Defu et al. *A Chinese-English Handbook of Idioms*. Hong Kong: Joint Publishing Co. 1986.

Weiner, Rebecca. *Living in China - A Guide to Teaching & Studying in China Including Taiwan*. San Francisco: China Books & Periodicals, Inc. 1991

Wu, Jingrong et al. *A Chinese-English Dictionary*. Beijing: Commercial Press, 1989.

About the author

James J. Wang was born, brought up, and educated in mainland China. He was a student at Beijing University from 1980-1984. After graduation, in1986-1987 he did literary research at the University of Massachusetts at Amherst as a scholar-in-residence. He then worked for five years as an English editor and translator in Beijing. In 1993 he returned to the United States and now works as freelance editor in San Francisco.